MW01169165

EP High School World History Printables: Levels 9-12

This book belongs to:

_____

This book was made for your convenience. It is available for printing from the Easy Peasy All-in-One Homeschool website. It contains all of the printables from Easy Peasy's High School World History course. The instructions for each page are found in the online course. THIS BOOK IS NOT A COMPLETE COURSE. The rest of the course is found online.

Easy Peasy All-in-One Homeschool is a free online homeschool curriculum providing high quality education for children around the globe. It provides complete courses for preschool through high school graduation. For EP's curriculum visit allinonehomeschool.com.

EP High School World History Printables: Levels 9-12

ISBN: 9798884062023

First Edition: March 2024

Grading Sheet: Quarter 1

World History

Record your scores on the sheet below as the assignments instruct you to do so.

Date	Lesson	Assignment	My Score	Possible Score
	2	Questions		12
	3	Paragraph		10
	5	Questions		24
	6	Paragraph		10
	8	Paragraph		10
	10	Paragraph		20
	13	Assignment		30
	14	Paragraph		10
	15	Paragraph		10
	16	Chart		12
	21	Presentation		40
	26	Paragraph		10
	29	Essay		40
	31	Map (potential for extra credit)		5
	32	Questions		10
	33	Questions		12
	33	Paragraphs		20
	34	Questions		12
	36	Questions		24
	38	Activity		12
	38	Paragraph		10
	42	Paragraphs		20
	44	Questions		23
	45	Chart (potential for extra credit)		40
		TOTAL		

Grading Sheet: Quarter 2

World History

Record your scores on the sheet below as the assignments instruct you to do so.

Date	Lesson	Assignment	My Score	Possible Score
	47	Essay		40
	49	Paragraph		20
	50	Paragraph		20
	51	Paragraph		20
	52	Paragraph		20
	53	Paragraph		20
	54	Paragraph		20
	55	Paragraph		10
	56	Paragraph		10
	57	Paragraph		20
	58	Chart		12
	64	Questions		5
	65	Paragraph		10
	67	Chart		24
	70	Essay		40
	71	95 Theses		24
	72	Paragraph		10
	73	Paragraph		10
	76	Paragraph		10
	79	Questions		8
	80	Questions		8
	81	Questions		4
	82	Questions		16
	83	Questions		16
	84	Questions		6
	85	Questions		4
	85	Chart (potential for extra credit)		35
	87	Question		2
	88	Questions		20
		TOTAL		

Grading Sheet: Quarter 3

World History

Record your scores on the sheet below as the assignments instruct you to do so.

Date	Lesson	Assignment	My Score	Possible Score
	94	Paragraph		10
	96	Paragraph		10
	100	Questions		62
	102	Assignment (possible extra credit)		24
	103	Paragraph		10
	106	Chart		10
	106	Project		15
	107	Paragraph		10
	109	Assignment		20
	111	Essay		40
	112	Paragraph		10
	113	Questions (possible extra credit)		10
	114	Questions (possible extra credit)		15
	115	Assignment		25
	118	Chart		10
	118	Paragraph		10
	126	Essay		40
	127	Quiz (possible extra credit)		15
	128	Questions		5
	129	Question		2
	129	WWI Poetry (possible extra credit)		20
	131	Assignment		12
	133	Assignment		14
	134	Assignment		20
		TOTAL		

Grading Sheet: Quarter 4

Record your scores on the sheet below as the assignments instruct you to do so.

Date	Lesson	Assignment	My Score	Possible Score
	139	Assignment		20
	141	Chart		20
	144	Paragraph		10
	153	Questions		30
	154	Paragraphs		30
	155	Timeline		10
	156	Chart		15
	157	Activity		20
	163	Paragraph		20
	165	Activity		40
	169	Essay		40
	172	Assignment		15
	173	Paragraph		20
	174	Questions		6
	176	Essay		40
	177	Questions		12
	180	Final Presentation		100
		TOTAL		

Lesson 1: Ancient River Valley Civilization Terms

1. **Nile River** – the river along which Ancient Egypt developed. Provided Egypt with protection, water and silt which fertilized the soil.

2. **Silt** – left behind on the soil after the Nile River flooded made the soil highly fertile for farming.

3. **Gift of the Nile** – the rich soil left behind after flooding and the prosperous farming that this led to.

4. **Irrigation** – the process of bringing water to crop fields.

5. **Hieroglyphics** – the Egyptian form of writing.

6. **Monarchy** – government headed by a king or a queen.

7. **Menes** – united Upper and Lower Egypt.

8. **Papyrus** – a plant that was made into paper on which Egyptians wrote.

9. **Pharaohs** – the rulers of Egypt.

10. **Dynasty** – a series of rulers from a single family.

11. **Old Kingdom** – also known as the Age of Pyramids time period where Egypt was ruled by pharaohs who were thought to be gods and when the majority of Egyptian pyramids were built.

12. **Middle Kingdom** – time period where pharaohs focused on projects that were good for the public transportation was improved, canals were dug for irrigation, etc. At the end of the Middle Kingdom, the Hyksos invaded and took control of Egypt.

13. **New Kingdom** – time period where Egypt established an empire by invading other lands and taking them over.

14. **Hyksos** – group who invaded Egypt during the Middle Kingdom.

15. **Late Kingdom** – period where Egypt suffered many invasions and lost most of its empire.

16. **Hatshepsut** – first female pharaoh.

17. **Akhenaton** – tried to convert Egyptians to monotheism from polytheism.

18. **Ramses II** – known for his building of temples and beautification of Egypt.

19. **Pyramids** – burial tombs for pharaohs.

20. **Lunar Calendar** – calendar based on the cycles of the moon.

21. **Fertile Crescent** – area within the Middle East that today is Israel, Jordan, Syria, Lebanon and Iraq.

22. **Tigris and Euphrates Rivers** – rivers along which the Fertile Crescent civilizations developed: provided water and irrigation but were also destructive when they flooded.

23. **Hammurabi** – created the first set of written laws.

24. **Babylonians** – people who Hammurabi ruled.

25. **Hammurabi's Code** – the first known written laws.

26. **Hittites** – the first people to learn to work with iron.

27. **Assyrians** – known to be the greatest warriors in the Fertile Crescent. Conquered the Babylonians.

28. **Chaldeans** – rebuilt Babylon and focused on creating a city of beauty.

29. **Nebuchadnezzar** – ruler of the Chaldeans who built the Hanging Gardens of Babylon.

30. **Persians** – created the largest empire in the ancient world.

31. **Phoenicians** – great sea traders and known for creating the first alphabet.

32. **Zoroastrianism** – the first religion to focus on the idea of heaven and hell/good vs. evil.

33. **Barter** – a form of trade in which people exchange goods not money.

34. **Hebrews** – created the empire of Israel after Moses led them out of Egypt. Eventually they became known as Jews and created the religion of Judaism. This was important because it made them the only monotheistic religious group in ancient times.

35. **Mosaic Law** – set of laws based on the teaching of Moses and the Ten Commandments.

36. **Judaism** – monotheistic religion that focused on following the Ten Commandments.

37. **Scribe** – professional writers.

38. **Civilization** – a complicated form of culture that has to include the growth of cities, specialized workers, writing, advanced technology and complex institutions like religion and government.

39. **Specialize** – to focus on a single job or task.

40. **Artisan** – skilled workers who specialized in their field of work like priests, teachers, scribes, etc.

41. **Surplus** – more than is needed.

42. **Cuneiform** – the Sumerian form of writing.

43. **Bronze** – mixture of copper and tin that is strong so weapons and tools became sturdier when they were made of bronze.

44. **Institution** – long last patterns of organization within a community.

45. **City state** – a city and all of the land that surrounds it.

46. **Ziggurat** – three-tiered temple found in Sumeria.

47. **Polytheist** – to believe in many gods.

48. **Empire** – to conquer other people and places and rule them.

49. **Colony** – a place governed/ruled by foreign people.

50. **Literacy** – the ability to read and write.

51. **Monotheist** – to believe in one god.

52. **Covenant** – a contract or pledge.

53. **Prophet** – a messenger sent to reveal God's will.

54. **Ethical Monotheism** – belief that proper moral conduct involves the worship of only one god.

55. **Satrap** – a royal governor of part of the Persian empire.

56. **Subcontinent** – a large region that is part of a continent, but is separated from the rest of the continent in some way.

57. **Monsoon** – seasonal wind.

58. **Reincarnation** – the belief that the soul is continually reborn.

59. **Moksha** – the state of perfect peace and understanding in Hinduism.

60. **Caste** – social class within Hinduism and ancient India.

61. **Karma** – the idea that a person's behavior in this life determines what caste they will be born into in their next life.

62. **Dharma** – the set of duties required of each caste in Hinduism.

63. **Nirvana** – the state of perfect peace and understanding in Buddhism.

64. **Ashoka** – Indian ruler who spread Buddhism to eastern Asia.

65. **Edict** – a public order or announcement that has authority.

66. **Mandate of Heaven** – in ancient China the belief that royal authority comes from the gods.

67. **Confucius** – Chinese philosopher who urged social harmony and good government through positive relationships.

68. **Chin Dynasty** – ruled China and built the Great Wall of China to protect China from invasion.

69. **Dynastic cycle** – a cycle of power and decline for Chinese dynasties.

70. **Loess** – fertile soil left behind by the flooding of the Huang He River.

71. **Oracle bones** – animal bones used by ancient Chinese priests to tell the future.

72. **Filial piety** – respect shown by children to their parents and elders.

(Terms from GAVL, creative commons 3.0 [https://creativecommons.org/licenses/by/3.0/], http://cms.gavirtualschool.org/Shared/SocialStudies/WorldHistory/AncRiverValleyCiv/WH_AncientRivValleyCiv_KeyTerms.pdf)

Lesson 1: Sumer Notes

What is a civilization? In order for a culture to be considered a civilization, it must possess all five of the following characteristics:
1. growth of cities
2. specialized workers
3. advanced technology
4. a form of writing
5. complex institutions like religion and government

What were the four main river valley civilizations?
1. Sumeria: formed around the Tigris and Euphrates Rivers
2. Egypt: formed around the Nile River
3. India: formed around the Indus and the Ganges Rivers
4. China: formed around the Hwang He River

Why did early civilizations develop around rivers?
1. Provided a source of water for the people
2. Provided a source of water to irrigate crops
3. When the rivers flooded they left behind nutrients in the soil that made the soil good for farming
4. Source of transportation

Sumer (Fertile Crescent)

Location: located in the Middle East along the Tigris and the Euphrates Rivers – today it would be Iraq, Lebanon, Syria, Jordan and Israel.

Geographic Advantages:
- Water source
- Fertile soil

Geographic Disadvantages and Solutions:
- Some years the rivers flooded to dangerous levels and destroyed homes, villages etc., while other years they did not flood at all and there were droughts.
  - Solution: people built their cities away from the rivers and built irrigation ditches to bring the water to the cities.
- The flat, bare land provided no natural defense against invasion (no trees, mountains, etc).
  - Solution: people built walls around their cities out of mud bricks which provided protection against invasion.

- Limited natural resources.
  - Solution: merchants traded their excess supply of food for the natural resources people needed. Traded their bronze tools and weapons to other groups of people. Bronze was much stronger than tin and copper which is what most people used to make tools and weapons so this was a valuable item for the Sumerians to trade.

Government: Priest-kings ruled Sumerian cities. The people believed that the kings had direct contact with the gods. Collected taxes and made offerings to the gods.

Religion: Polytheistic (believed in many gods). Sumerians believed that the gods controlled all aspects of life and when good or bad things happened it was because the gods were either pleased or displeased.

Society: Sumer was divided into social classes – priests were the highest, wealthy merchants were next, farmers and artisans third and slaves were last. Sumerian women had many rights and could participate in most occupations.

People of the Fertile Crescent:
1. **Sumerians**: first known civilization in the Fertile Crescent; created Cuneiform or the first form of writing in this region

2. **Amorites/Babylonians**: defeated Sumeria, ruled by Hammurabi and were responsible for the first written set of laws.

3. **Hittites**: lived in Fertile Crescent and were the first people to learn how to use iron to make weapons and tools – this made them stronger and made them last longer than when they were made with bronze.

4. **Phoenicians**: great sea traders and created the first alphabet.

5. **Hebrews/Jews**: they were different from other people at the time because they were monotheistic (believed in one god). Moses led the Jews out of Egypt to the Fertile Crescent where they established the kingdom of Israel. Lived by a covenant with God which was outlined in the Ten Commandments.

6. **Assyrians**: greatest warriors in the Fertile Crescent because of their emphasis on military training and weaponry. Eventually they were defeated by the Chaldeans.

7. **Chaldeans**: made Babylon their capital and rebuilt it beautifully. Ruled by Nebuchadnezzar and he built the Hanging Gardens of Babylon. Conquered the Jews and kept many of them captive in Babylon (known as the Babylonian Captivity). However, the Jews kept their religious beliefs and refused to convert to polytheism.

8. **Persians**: ruled the largest empire in the ancient world. Divided their empire into 20 provinces which were each ruled by a satrap (a royal governor). They also built amazing road systems and standardized their money system. Zoroaster (a Persian) was the first person outside of the Jews to bring up the idea that people controlled their own fate through the decisions they made. He taught about right vs. wrong, good vs. evil, and heaven vs. hell.

Lesson 4: Ancient Egypt Notes

Location: along the Nile River in present-day Egypt.

Geographic Advantages:
1. Nile provided water
2. Nile provided fertile soil for farming
3. Nile provided transportation
4. Deserts, rugged coastlines, the Nile, the Red Sea and the Mediterranean Sea protected Egypt from invasion

Government: Upper and Lower Egypt were united by Menes and he began the system of dynasties (a series of rulers from the same family). Egypt was ruled by pharaohs who were believed to be gods.

Religion: Polytheistic. Pharaohs were thought to be gods and were buried in pyramids. Originally it was believed that only pharaohs could hope for pleasant afterlives – everyone else was doomed to misery and sorrow. Over time, though, this idea changed and it was believed that everyone was entitled to a prosperous afterlife.

History:
- **Old Kingdom**: also known as the "Age of Pyramids" because this is when most pyramids were built. Pharaohs were glorified. 2660-2180 B.C. Ended when the First Illness occurred – poor harvests, warfare and lawlessness. People lost faith in the pharaohs because they thought the First Illness happened because the gods were unhappy with the pharaohs.

- **Middle Kingdom**: 2080-1640 B.C. Pharaohs restored power and moved the capital to Thebes. Focused on projects for the public trying to keep the people happy. Encouraged trade, improved transportation, built irrigation canals and made sure all people had plenty to eat. A Second Illness occurred, though, and a group of people from the East (the Hyksos) invaded Egypt and took over. They were able to conquer Egypt because they had horse-drawn carriages and weapons the Egyptians had never seen before.

- **Rule of the Hyksos**: 1640-1570 B.C. Eventually overthrown by the Egyptians and pharaohs are restored to power.

- **New Kingdom**: 1570-1075 B.C. Egypt decided to avoid invasion by invading those around them. Egypt creates an empire.

- **Late Period**: 1075-671 B.C. Period of decline for Egypt. They lost their empire and faced many invasions.

Pharaohs:
1. Menes: United Upper and Lower Egypt
2. Hatshepsut: first female pharaoh
3. Ramses II: known for building great temples
4. Akhenaton: tried to convert Egyptians from polytheism to monotheism – not successful for long

Social Classes: great differences between the upper and lower classes
- **Upper class**: pharaoh, pharaoh's family and advisors, nobles, priests – lived in large homes, had plenty to eat, held extravagant banquets, many clothes, jewels.
- **Lower Class**: peasants – worked hard in the fields and paid high taxes

Cultural Advancements:
- Writing: hieroglyphics – wrote on papyrus
- Numeral system for accounting
- Geometry to build pyramids
- Lunar Calendar: 12 months with 30 days each
- Medicine: first to perform brain surgery and make accurate drawings of human organs

Lesson 7: Indus River Valley Notes

Location: along the Indus and the Ganges Rivers – called a subcontinent of Asia because it is separated from the rest of Asia by the Himalayan Mountains

Geographic Advantages:
1. Water from the rivers
2. Fertile soil
3. Natural protection from mountains and the Indian Ocean

Geographic Disadvantage: Monsoons brought destructive flooding sometimes and horrible droughts other times.

Cities: well-planned and organized (grid system for paved roads, multi-story homes with running water, garbage collection systems, etc.). Mohenjo-Daro and Harappa are the two most famous. Both declined and disappeared and no one is truly sure why.

Hinduism:
- The one true reality is Brahman, the mighty spirit that creates and destroys.
- All wise Hindus try to reach moksha: a state of perfect understanding.
- You reach moksha by going through reincarnation, or a rebirth of the spirit into new lives.
- This led to the formation of castes or social classes: Brahmin (priests), Kshatriyas (rulers and warriors), Vaishyas (landowners, merchants and artisans), Shudras (slaves). Castes could not intermingle with one another – they were strictly separated.
- Taught karma which is the idea that your actions in this life determine what caste you will be born into in your next life.
- Also taught dharma which is the duties that each caste must fulfill in their lifetime.

Buddhism: some people rejected Hinduism because of the caste system and began to follow Siddhartha Gautama or Buddha.
- Four Noble Truths: all of life is suffering and sorrow, the cause of this suffering and sorrow is people's selfish desires, the way to end suffering and sorrow is to end all selfish desires, you can end selfish desires by following the Eightfold Path.
- The Eightfold Path led to nirvana – release from pain and sorrow.

(From GAVL, creative commons 3.0 [https://creativecommons.org/licenses/by/3.0/], http://cms.gavirtualschool.org/Shared/
SocialStudies/WorldHistory/AncRiverValleyCiv/AncientIndiaNotes.pdf)

Location: along the Huang He River

Geographic Advantages:
1. Water from the rivers
2. Fertile soil
3. Protection from invasion by mountains, deserts and oceans

Government:
- China was ruled by emperors who came from dynasties.
- Emperors were thought to have the Mandate of Heaven, or the approval of the gods so people followed them devoutly.
- Edicts were public order or announcement that has authority

Beliefs: family was the center of all Chinese society. Respect for parents and elders is referred to as Filial Piety.

Writing system: calligraphy (a series of characters)

Chinese teachings:
1. Confucianism: advocated social harmony through relationships and good government
2. Taoism: founded by Lao Tzu; people should follow nature's "harmony"

Powerful dynasties:
1. Ch'in (or Qin): built the Great Wall of China
2. Han: opened trade along the Great Silk Road

Lesson 11: Ancient Hebrew Notes

The ancient Hebrews are the only surviving nation of people who lived in the Fertile Crescent. Today, they are known as Jews.

The Promised Land:
According to the Bible, God appeared to a nomad named Abraham. God promised to give Abraham and his descendants a land of their own if they worshipped only Him (around 1500BC) After years of wandering the desert, they eventually settled in the land of Canaan (modern day Israel), which was "flowing with milk and honey." Around 1400BC, the Jews migrated to Egypt to work for the invading Hyksos. After about 100 years, the Hyksos were kicked out of Egypt, and the Jews (Hebrews) were made slaves in Egypt.

The Exodus: Moses led the enslaved Hebrews out of Egypt around 1200BC. The Hebrews were the slaves of the pharaoh, probably Ramses II. The word, "Exodus" means departure. Before the pharaoh set the Hebrews free, several plagues afflicted Egypt.

Plagues:
1. Nile River turned to blood.
2. Frogs
3. Lice
4. Flies
5. Livestock pestilence
6. Boils
7. Hail/meteors
8. Locusts
9. Eclipse
10. Angel of Death

Passover: The Hebrews were instructed to sacrifice a lamb and paint its blood over their door to prevent the Angel of Death from killing their first-born child. Passover is still celebrated today by modern-day Jews to remember this event from their history.

Other notes:
- King David (dad) and King Solomon (son) were two Hebrew kings. Before David was a king, he was a shepherd. He fought Goliath. King Solomon was known for his wisdom and the palaces he built.
- The Hebrew kingdoms were Israel in the north and Judah in the south. (around 900BC)

Monotheism: Belief in one God

Polytheism: Belief in many Gods

Torah: "law," the first five books of the Bible.

Tabernacle: A shrine or place of worship.

Covenant: An agreement

Examples of a covenant:
- Noah and the ark
- Moses and the Ten Commandments which he received on Mt. Sinai

(From GAVL, creative commons 3.0 [https://creativecommons.org/licenses/by/3.0/], http://cms.gavirtualschool.org/Shared/
SocialStudies/WorldHistory/AncRiverValleyCiv/HebrewNotes.pdf)

Lesson 14: Ancient Greek Terms

1. **Western Civilization** – Greek ideas that spread to Europe and America and remain a part of our culture.

2. **Aegean Sea** – sea that surrounds mainland Greece.

3. **Mediterranean Sea** – large sea that the Aegean Sea opens into.

4. **Socrates** – a famous Greek philosopher who questioned all of the accepted values in Greece. He created a form of teaching that involved asking question after question (the Socratic Method).

5. **Black Sea** – east of Greece and united Greece with the eastern world.

6. **Tyrants** – ambitious men who came to power through rebellions. They supported the wants/needs of the common people rather than the nobles.

7. **Aristocracy** – a government run by a small group of noble/wealthy families.

8. **Cleisthenes** – he enacted a series of laws that made Athens a full democracy. He created the Council of 500 and allowed citizens to serve on the Council. He also increased the power of the Athenian assembly.

9. **Sparta** – Greek city-state that focused solely on its military and military domination.

10. **Peloponnesus** – the southern part of Greece where Sparta was located.

11. **Pericles** – ruled Athens for many years. Pericles increased the number of public officials in Athens, strengthened democracy in Athens by increasing the number of paid officials, and he gained wealth for Athens through the Delian League.

12. **Council of 500** – this group was made up of Athenian citizens and was supposed to propose laws and advise the assembly on what actions to take.

13. **Delian League** – this was an alliance of 140 city-states and was headed by Athens. Their purpose was to ward off further attacks by the Persians by uniting all of Greece.

14. **Ephor** – these were the rulers of Sparta. They had unlimited power and they used it harshly. The forbade any citizens from leaving Sparta and they did not allow outsiders to visit Sparta.

15. **Archon** – these were the early rulers of Athens.

16. **Democracy** – this is a form of government in which all citizens take part.

17. **Comedy** – this is a play that made fun of people, politics and ideas of the time.

18. **Tragedy** – this is a play that had men and women of strong character. Eventually their strength led to their downfall.

19. **Alexander the Great** – this man created the largest empire of the time that was headed by Greece and created a blended culture called Hellenism.

20. **Orators** – public speakers.

21. **Plato** – he was a student of Socrates and he believed that society should be ruled by the greatest philosophers, not democracy. He believed that average citizens were not educated enough to govern wisely.

22. **Aristotle** – he believed that all truths followed logically from other truths. In other words, people should use general logic to make decisions. Here is an example:
    a. all people are mortal.
    b. Socrates was a person.
    c. Therefore, Socrates was mortal.
        • Everything followed logic.

23. **Homer** – this man was famous for his epics.

24. **Herodotus** – he was the first true historian.

25. **Philosophers** – these people questioned the most basic and widely accepted ideas of the time in the search for truth.

26. **Drama** – written plays to be performed on stage. Created by the Greeks.

27. **Agora** – a marketplace where Greek people gathered.

28. **Polis** – the Greek word for city-state.

29. **City-state** – a city surrounded by a wall and all of the land surrounding that city.

30. **Chora** – the land outside of the city walls as part of a city-state.

31. **Acropolis** – a fortified hilltop.

1. **Republic** – government elected by citizen.

2. **Proletariat** – "the mass of poor people" in Roman cities.

3. **Plebian** – Roman lower classes.

4. **Civil War** – war between rival groups of the same country.

5. **Veto** – a rejection of a proposed law.

6. **Gravitas** – "seriousness" of Roman character.

7. **Patrician** – Roman upper class and wealthy people.

8. **Triumvirate** –group of three powerful men in Rome.

9. **Monarchy** – rule by king or queen.

10. **Senate** – governing body of Rome

11. **Mercenary** – a "hired" soldier, usually hired from another country.

12. **Tribune** – elected leader of Rome's lower class.

13. **Legion** – the Roman army.

14. **Consul** – elected for one-year terms by Senators to govern the Republic.

15. **Dictator** – elected by Senate in times of crisis. Given absolute authority.

16. **Gladiator** – slave trained to fight to the death for Roman entertainment.

17. **Civil service** – handles the day-to-day running of a government

18. **Stoicism** – encouraged strength, duty, and loyalty. Main philosophy of Romans.

19. **Apostle** – follower of Jesus of Nazareth. Literally, "sent one."

20. **Bishop** – official appointed to run a geographical area of the Catholic Church

21. **Policy** – rules set up by government or an organization.

22. **Succession** – rules for determining who becomes ruler when one ruler dies.

23. **Satire** – plays that poked fun of Roman politicians and celebrities.

24. **Messiah** – a "savior." Jesus of Nazareth was an example.

25. **Pope** – head of the Roman Catholic Church

26. **Aqueduct** – invention of the Romans to control water flow into the cities.

27. **Epicureanism** – philosophy of Romans that emphasized pleasure over pain.

28. **Villa** – Wealthy Roman estate in the country side.

29. **Martyr** – person who dies for a cause or religion.

Geography:

Three fourths of Greece is covered with rugged mountain ranges. These mountains separated the people of Greece and led to the formation of isolated city-states with widely varied cultures, ideas and values. There was no sense of unity in Greece because of this separation. Greece also had no major rivers to rely on so people had to live close to the sea.

Food and Trade: The climate in Greece was mild and allowed for good soil and enough rainfall to grow grapes and olives. The people traveled by sea to other places to trade grapes and olives for meat, cloth, tools, weapons, etc. Greeks also relied on the sea for fishing which was another source of food.

Early History of Greece:

1. **Minoans** (2000-1400BC): lived on the island of Crete and were ruled by King Minos. They built powerful ships and were known as great traders. Disappeared due to either a powerful tidal wave or volcanic eruption.

2. **Mycenaeans** (1600-1200BC): built the first city-states. They were the first Greeks to use bronze to build stronger weapons and tools.

3. **Dorians** (1200-700BC): illiterate people who did little to advance Greek culture.

Lesson 16: Golden Age Greece Notes

Greek Mythology:
1. People believed that religion could explain:
   - Mysteries like thunder, rain, change of season, etc. In other words, the gods made all of this happen if they were pleased or displeased with the Greek people
   - How to make the gods happy so that the Greek people could gain long life, good fortune, abundant harvests, etc.

2. Greek gods were thought to have human characteristics and weaknesses. All gods and goddesses lived on top of Mount Olympus and Zeus was the king of all gods. The Greeks created myths, or traditional stories, about the deeds and misdeeds of the gods and goddesses.

3. Religious practices included:
   - Visits to oracles: these were temples where the gods and goddesses spoke to citizens through priests.
   - Olympic Games: athletic contests in honor of the gods and goddesses.

Greek Rulers:
1. **Nobles**: From 700-650 BC, Greece was ruled by nobles. They created city-states and controlled most of the land. People could rent land from them to farm or rent land to become merchants. Nobles encouraged all of discontented people to move to other places. This is how Greece formed colonies. Colonies allowed Greek culture to spread to other parts of the world and they promoted trade. Colonies imported/bought Greek grapes and olives and exported/sold grains and other goods to mainland Greece.

2. **Tyrants**: 650-500BC. Took power by force and wanted to improve the lives of the common people. Began to establish the idea of democracy (a government in which all people rule themselves).

3. **Democratic governments**: eventually tyrants lost power and city-states turned to democracy.

Athens and Sparta: The two most-powerful Greek city-states.
1. Sparta:
   - Culture was based on a strong military.

- Citizens were native men, "neighbors" were free people who lived in Sparta but they were not natives of Sparta – they had moved there from other places, helots were slaves in Sparta.
- Ephors (military leaders) led the government of Sparta.
- The government/military regulated the lives of all Spartan citizens.
- Men were to serve in the military and women were to run households and have children. All boys went to begin military training at age 7 and they served in the military until they turned 60.
- As a result of this, Spartans sacrificed individual freedom for the good of the city-state and Sparta created nothing in terms of art, literature, etc.

2. Athens:
   - A city-state of sea traders.
   - Citizens were native men, "metics" were free people who were not originally from Athens – usually they were merchants or artisans, and last Athens had slaves.
   - Archons ruled Athens – they were elected by the Athenian people.
   - Athens created much in the way of drama, literature, art, architecture, etc.

Persian Wars: In 546BC, Persia attacked Greece and Greece and Persia then fought a series of wars until 479BC. Eventually Greece defeated Persia. This was important because it gave the Greeks a feeling of military superiority, it allowed them to create an empire because they took control of many Persian lands, and it united the Greeks in defense of their lands. Athens also emerged as a great military city-state after these wars because their army performed much better than any others in Greece (including the Spartans!).

Delian League: 140 Greek city-states united to form the Delian League. Their purpose was to stay united in order to ward off another Persian attack. Athens led the Delian League and each city-state contributed money, ships, weapons and soldiers to the Delian League.

Lesson 16: Athens vs. Sparta Chart

	Athens	Sparta
Location in Greece		
Focus in Society		
Form of Government (give a description)		
Views on the Role of Women in Society		
Cultural Additions to Greek Society		
Attitudes/Values		

Philip of Macedon:

Philip of Macedon invaded Greece in the 350s BC. He created the first paid army made up of foot soldiers called an infantry and soldiers on horseback called a cavalry. He was the first person to unite Greece into one large empire under one ruler. When Philip died, his son Alexander became the ruler of Greece.

Alexander the Great:

Alexander conquered lands all the way to India and created the largest Greek empire of all. He also created a Hellenistic culture (what he's most famous for) throughout his entire empire.

Characteristics of Hellenistic culture:

- Carefully planned cities with markets, theatres, schools and gyms
- Women were considered citizens
- Strong focus on ethics and values
- Math and physics were studied in great detail
- Medicine was improved and anesthesia was used for the first time – the brain was also studied in detail
- Astronomy and geography were studied in detail as well

(From GAVL, creative commons 3.0 [https://creativecommons.org/licenses/by/3.0/], http://cms.gavirtualschool.org/Shared/SocialStudies/WorldHistory/AncientGreeksRomans/AlexanderNotes.pdf)

Lesson 22: Roman Republic Notes

Geography of Italy: Rome is found on the western coast of the Italian peninsula. This location was beneficial to Rome because it gave the Romans access to the Mediterranean Sea and the Tiber River. The sea and the river were used for water sources, irrigation, and trade. Italy has a few mountain ranges but they can be easily traveled.

Settlement: Rome was settled by the Latins, the Greeks and the Etruscans.

Government and Society: Rome created a republic, a society where citizens with the right to vote choose their leaders. This is different from a democracy because in a democracy ALL people can vote in a republic only some people can vote.

Romans valued family and gravitas (strength and seriousness) above all other things. Families were headed by the eldest male, however, the opinions of women were valued. Women did NOT have the right to vote, though.

Roman men were divided into social classes:
- **Patricians** were the privileged upper class. Their ancestors were said to have originally founded Rome. Patricians were citizens with the right to vote and the authority to make laws. Patricians held all political offices.
- The common farmers, merchants and artisans were **plebians**. Plebians had the right to vote but they could not hold political office.

Roman religion was very similar to Greek religion. The Romans borrowed the Greek gods and goddesses as their own. The Romans gave the Greek gods and goddesses new names but their personalities and myths remained the same.

Rome also created an army and began to conquer lands around them this created a large Roman Empire.

Balanced Government: Over time plebians became unhappy with not being able to hold political offices. Plebians made up the majority of the Roman army, so they refused to serve in the army until they were given more political power. As a result, several political reforms took place:

1. **Twelve Tables**: all Roman laws were written so that everyone could read them and understand them. The laws were equally applied to

patricians and plebians.

2. **The office of Consul** was created: two consuls ruled Rome (almost like kings) they could veto decisions made by the Senate and the Assembly

3. **The Senate** was created: usually senators were patricians and they were in charge of creating foreign and domestic policy

4. **The Assembly** was created: made up of plebians and their primary task was to make laws

The Punic Wars:
1. First Punic War: Rome and Carthage went to war over Sicily. Carthage had a huge army and a huge navy but Rome still had the advantage. Romes army was large and it was more loyal than Carthage's army. Carthage used mercenaries in their army, whereas Rome used Roman citizens. This usually meant that the Romans were more loyal to their army. Rome also copied Carthage's ships and built a huge navy. Rome won this war.

2. Second Punic War: Carthage invaded Rome led by Hannibal. They attacked Rome from the north, and they were able to destroy most of Italy. However, Rome was able to defend itself and not be destroyed. Rome sent an army to attack Carthage which meant Hannibal had to send some of his troops back to Carthage to defend the homeland. As a result, Rome won this war.

3. Third Punic War: Rome attacked Carthage and destroyed the city.

Results of the Punic Wars:
- Many Roman soldiers died
- The homes of most soldiers had been destroyed in the Second Punic War and they could not afford to rebuild their homes
- Most patricians/landowners chose to use slaves for workers rather than hire out of work soldiers because they didn't have to pay slaves anything
- This new class of landless, poor became known as the proletariat

Attempts at Reform: After the Punic Wars left many landless and poor, there were many attempts at reform.

- The Gracchi: Tiberius and Gaius Gracchus tried to convince the Assembly to distribute all land in Rome equally. This way there would not be a huge gap between the patricians and the proletariat. Senators clubbed him to death before his ideas could be passed into law.

- Julius Caesar: 44 BC Caesar is named dictator of Rome for 10 years. He made himself the head of the Senate and allowed plebians to serve in the Senate. He forced landowners to use free men for 1/3 of their workers (this meant the proletariat had jobs open to them); he adopted a 365-day calendar; he gave land to the poor; and he created many new public jobs for the poor. In 44 BC, he was murdered by senators who feared that he was taking too much power away from them.

- Octavian Caesar: 27 BC he is named Augustus or "the exalted one" and is made sole ruler of Rome. His rule is known as the Pax Romana or the period of peace and prosperity. Augustus encouraged trade, created a single currency (the denarius) for the entire Roman empire, built aqueducts to bring water into Rome, built roads and structures out of concrete so that they would last for centuries, and he created a civil service where anyone could apply to work in a government/ political position.

Rome and Christianity: In AD 6, Rome conquered Israel and took the Jews under their control. Within 24 years, the teachings of Jesus began to spread throughout this region. Jesus taught that God was the one true ruler and that people should follow the Ten Commandments in their lives as their laws. He also taught that wealth was not important or impressive and it didn't say anything about a person's status in the world. Many Roman leaders feared Jesus because they believed that the Roman people would revolt and want him to become their new leader. Jesus was crucified in AD 30. Christianity continued to spread throughout Rome after Jesus' death. In AD 313, the ruler Constantine welcomed Christians in the Roman empire and allowed all people to choose their own religion.

Lesson 26: Fall of Rome Notes

The Fall of the Roman Empire: In AD 476, Rome's empire officially ceased to exist. Many things caused this loss of power:

1. Roman soldiers were no longer loyal to the rulers of Rome; they thought only about the pay they received.

2. Political rulers were no longer revered by the people because of conflicts over the gap between the rich and the poor and the Christian faith.

3. Inflation caused Rome's money to become worthless.

4. People were no longer patriotic.

5. Germanic tribes began to invade Rome.

(From GAVL, creative commons 3.0 [https://creativecommons.org/licenses/by/3.0/], http://cms.gavirtualschool.org/Shared/
SocialStudies/WorldHistory/AncientGreeksRomans/FallOfRomeNotes.pdf)

Lesson 31: Byzantine Empire Notes World History

The Fall of the Roman Empire:
- Had broken into East and West for management purposes.

    1. West invaded by Barbarians and broken down

    2. East Ousts Barbarians under Emperor Justinian
        - Justinian begins political, economic, intellectual, and artistic revival that will keep Byzantine Empire strong for more than 1000 years.

The Byzantine Empire:
- The Church

    1. Recognized the Patriarch in Constantinople rather than the Pope in Rome as head of the Church

    2. After years of arguments, the Christian Church split in 1054.
        - West – Roman Catholic
        - East – Eastern Orthodox

- Byzantine Culture

    1. Preserved Roman Law
        - Justinian ordered scholars to collect and organize all Roman Law. This collection of laws is known as Justinian's Code.
            - It remained in force until the Ottoman Turks toppled the empire in 1453.

Lesson 33: Byzantine Video Questions

1. How did Constantine the Great become emperor?

2. What obstacle did Constantine have to overcome before he became sole emperor?

3. What event occurred before Constantine's battle with Maxentius?

4. In what year did Constantine overcome Maxentius and become sole emperor?

5. Following his victory over Maxentius, Constantine made two critical decisions; what were they?

6. In what year did Constantine establish Constantinople, and what is that city called today?

(From GAVL, creative commons 3.0 [https://creativecommons.org/licenses/by/3.0/], http://cms.gavirtualschool.org/Shared/SocialStudies/ WorldHistory/ByzantineIslamMongol/ByzantineVideoQuestions.pdf)

Lesson 34: Mongol Questions

1. What were the origins of the Mongols?

2. What was Genghis Khan's significance?

3. What were the Mongols effects on overland trade?

4. Who was Marco Polo and what was his significance?

5. Who was the leader of the Yuan Dynasty in China?

6. What was the Mongols' effect on Russia?

Lesson 40: Development of Africa Notes

Pre-European African and American Societies – The Development of Africa (100-1500)

Geography: Geographic features in Sub-Sahara Africa created a self-contained environment. It was and is the 2nd largest continent, covering 20% of earth's land surface. There are 5 distinct geographic regions:

1. **Northern and Southern coasts**: narrow strips of fertile land/ moderate rainfall and warm temperatures.
2. **Deserts**: Sahara and Kalahari – 1/3 of Africa's land.
   - Sahara: Atlantic Ocean to Red Sea, area roughly the size of the U.S. Not totally arid. 90 inhabited oases (an oasis is a place where underground water comes to the surface in a spring or well), caravans followed a fixed route.
3. **Dry Grasslands**: Too dry for farming, but sustainable for grazing. Delicate balance between people and animals.
4. **Savanna**: tall grass plains. During rainy seasons things come alive. Farming is difficult because rains strip the soil of minerals and in the dry season the ground is hard.
5. **Rain Forest**: damp, densely wooded region with Africa's second longest river, the Zaire, twisting through it. Little undergrowth due to huge mahogany and teak trees.

The sub-Saharan regions are home to the tsetse fly, a deadly bug which has played a major role in history. Its presence has kept traders and missionaries away, as well as farmers that couldn't bring livestock near.

Geography contained Africa:
- Dangerous rivers with rapids and falls
- Smooth coastline with few harbors and bays
- Tricky currents
- Difficult wind conditions
- Vast distances combined with deserts and rainforests limit travel and trade

Kush: Kush was the first major kingdom of sub-Sahara Africa its capital was Meroë. Kush adopted Egyptian ideas, hieroglyphics, pyramid building. Their ambitious traders traded their iron ore (iron tools they made) for luxury items like jewelry, fine cotton cloth, silver lamps, and glass bottles. Historical details about many aspects of life in Meroë are limited, and the reasons for its collapse are unknown. Historians are certain that the rising power of Axum was a decisive cause.

Axum: Axum was the capital of a kingdom located in a plateau region of eastern Africa called Ethiopia. It grew rich by controlling trade between African interior and the Red Sea Rulers. Axum became Christian in 324 AD. When Islamic armies swept through, they remained unconquered and unconverted. This ended the contact between kings and Christian lands of Western Europe and the Byzantine Empire. (In 1520 a Portuguese explorer journeyed into Ethiopian highlands and was amazed to find Christians worshiping in beautiful rock churches.)

Coastal Cities (Swahili city-states): East African coast city-states developed with names like Malindi, Mombasa, and Zanzibar because Arab Muslims lived on the coast. Over centuries two people groups, Bantu and Arab, inter-married. Their cultures blended and formed a new culture known as Swahili (from an Arabic term meaning people of the coast). They spoke Swahili and the major religion was Islam. Most lived by farming, fishing, and trading with Asia. The most common ship in a Swahili harbor was a triangular Arab vessel called dhows (pronounced dowz). It was large enough to carry profitable cargo, but sturdy enough to withstand the monsoon winds of the Indian Ocean. Arabs were middlemen in the Indian Ocean and brought Asian luxuries to Africa and African luxuries to Asia.

The Swahili Coast of Africa consisted of independent city-states where the leader was supreme in this time period. Swahili was a common culture of these people, and a merging of Bantu and Arabic beliefs. Kilwa was an important one of these city-states. Kilwa was the farthest south you could go in one monsoon season. People from South Africa would bring goods to Kilwa and trade with merchants participating in the Indian Ocean trade network. Kilwa grew to be a very large cosmopolitan trading city.

The Swahili Coast city-states were affected a lot by Islam. The form of Islam that affected the Swahili Coast city-states was a much purer form of Islam than what was practiced in sub-Saharan Africa. The reason for this is that the Swahili Coast city-states were in constant contact with Arabia through trading.

One of the most important historical effects of the Swahili Coast trade network is how it nurtured the Indian Ocean trade network. Merchants would travel from the East Asian zone of the trade network with Asian spices and wait for the next monsoon season to bring them back to Arabia and Africa. Once they arrived in Africa, they would trade their cargoes of spices for gold, ivory, and slaves. The Swahili Coast states often traded with a civilization inside of Africa, such as Great Zimbabwe, to get these items. The merchant would then wait for the next monsoon season to bring them back to Asia.

Swahili Coast trade would continue until the early 1500s when Portuguese ships entered Indian Ocean trade. The Portuguese easily defeated the city-states, which never needed any large armies or forts before. Merchants had always been safe, so the city-states were unprepared for the Portuguese attack.

Zimbabwe Became a Kingdom: Most gold and ivory that was traded came from Zimbabwe. It had inland location protection from Muslim influence. In Zimbabwe was built an impressive residence known as Great Zimbabwe that towered proudly over surrounding savanna. Zimbabwe reached its peak in early the 1400s. The arrival of the Portuguese in 1500s shattered their kingdom.

West African Empires Thrive on Trade: Three powerful empires developed in Western Africa (between the Sahara and the tropical rainforest in the savannas) between 300 and 1600: Ghana, Mali, and Songhai.

Gold came from the forest region south of the savanna between the Niger and Senegal rivers. Miners worked in secrecy. Until 1350 at least 2/3 of the world's supply of gold came from West Africa.

Although rich in gold, they lacked salt. In contrast, the Sahara contained abundant deposits of salt. They even built the sides of their houses with it. Merchants from both places would travel to trading centers like Jenne (pronounced je-NAY) and Timbuktu. They would exchange goods under watchful eye of tax collector.

Some traders took part in silent trade. Arab traders would bring salt, beat drums inviting gold merchants to trade, then ride off a few miles. Gold traders would arrive, look over the salt, and leave some of their gold and then hide. The Arabs would come back and decide whether enough gold had been left. If they thought not they would beat drums again, inviting a second round of trading. All of this occurred without ever speaking to each other.

Ghana's ruler demanded taxes and gifts of chiefs from surrounding lands. As long as payments were made, they were left in peace. Ghana's kingdom rose and shrank with the strength of its leader. Ghana was the only one allowed to own gold nuggets to control the price of gold. They were overrun by Muslim Berbers from the North, never to regain their power.

Malinthe Mandingo controlled the gold trade. A ruthless king, he ruled and killed 11 of 12 of his rival's sons. This proved to be a huge mistake. That son grew to be strong and defeated him. He promoted agriculture and gold-salt trade and named his kingdom Mali.

Influenced by Muslim traders, some of Mali's next rulers became Muslims. Under Mansa Musa (Mali's 9th Mansa), Mali became the most powerful empire that dominated West Africa.

Eventually, existing mines gave out and the trade routes shifted eastward. By the 1450s, the Songhai people replaced the Mandingo as controllers of the trade routes. Songhai had two great kings, one a ruthless conqueror and one an excellent administrator who set up an efficient tax system. However, they lacked gunpowder and cannons and were conquered by a Moroccan sultan.

Africans shared a cultural pattern:
Families were organized in groups called lineages. This included past generations and future generations. Some took the place of kings or other rulers. These felt strong loyalty to one another. The society passed down values and traditions through oral history.

Women were workers who planted and harvest crops and occasionally took an active part in commerce and trade. Men dominated government, but some women could become head of state in a few African kingdoms. In some societies, children traced their ancestors through their mothers rather than their fathers. This is known as a matrilineal system. They inherited land or wealth from their mother's brothers.

Religions blended monotheism and polytheism. Most honored a large number of gods and spirits, but believed this High God or Supreme Spirit was too powerful and distant to listen to human appeals. The spirits of departed ancestors were especially important. They believed these spirits could bring trouble or good fortune. At least one member of the village was trained in communicating with the spirit's "diviner." They called on the spirits whenever there was an illness or crisis.

Art Flourished:

Art linked religion, politics, and every day life. Some honored the king or the spirits of their ancestors. They used beautifully grained woods that grew there to create sculptures. Metalworking led to striking sculpture in gold and bronze. Some of the most famous African sculptures were created by the Yoruba group of people in the rainforest of what is now Nigeria.

Music and dance were also popular. The music had very complex rhythms and was known as "polyrhythmic." It often accompanied dancers who wore masks to honor the spirits or family ancestors. The art of carved masks, the music of the drums, and the dancing of the villagers shared a common purpose. They bound a community together and enabled it to pass on its heritage through the centuries.

Most African countries had no writing systems. Instead, each group handed down its history and laws by word of mouth. In many West African societies, specially trained people known as griots (pronounced GREE-ohz) were the record-keepers. Even after Arab traders brought Arabic writing, griots remained the historians of their people.

Lesson 40: Early African/Meso-American Terms World History

Bantu

1. **Sub-Sahara** – geographical area of Africa below the Sahara Desert.
2. **Oasis** – area in deserts that are abundant in water and plants.
3. **Semiarid** – area such as the Sahara Desert that gets very little annual rainfall.
4. **Desertification** – the process of an area "becoming" a desert.
5. **Savanna** – a plain area covered with grasses and ponds.
6. **Swahili** – an African language traced back to the Bantu peoples.
7. **Dhow** – Arab sailing vessel on the East Cost of Africa.
8. **Lineage** – one's family line.
9. **Matrilineal** – clans where the mother and the mother's family is dominant.
10. **Diviner** – an African tribal priest who talked to the spirit world.
11. **Griot** – African Tribal record keepers.
12. **Bantu** – early African tribes that migrated and settled the African continent.

Olmecs and Mayans

13. **Calendar** – major achievement of the Mayans.
14. **Central America** – geographic area between North and South America.
15. **Civilization** – a culture that has developed a form of government, religion, and learning.
16. **Cultural diffusion** – the spread of culture through trade.
17. **Culture** – a social group's habits, customs, and traditions.
18. **Jaguar** – highly visible in Olmec art; often drawn as the rain god.
19. **The Olmecs** – earliest American culture in Mexico; thrived around 1500 BC.
20. **Number system** – developed by Olmecs to keep record of traded items.

Incas and Aztecs

21. **Calpulli** – groups of Aztec families each with their own temple and school.

22. **Chinampas** – highly fertile gardens created by the Aztecs in the shallow lakes around their settlements.

23. **Cortes** – Leader of the Spanish army that conquered the Aztecs.

24. **Jaguars** – Aztecs' finest warriors.

25. **Moctezuma** – one of the great Aztec rulers.

26. **Sacrifice** – killing an animal or person as an offering to the gods.

27. **Tenochtitlan** – the capital of the Aztecs, founded in 1325 and built on an island in Lake Texcoco.

28. **Tribute** – a form of tax paid to the Aztec ruler by the people living in the towns throughout the Aztec Empire.

29. **Cuzco** –capital city of the Incan Empire.

30. **Andes** – mountain chain in South America that was home to the Incas

31. **Machu Pichu** – a major Incan city full of temples.

32. **Pizarro** – Spanish conqueror of the Incas.

1. What are the 5 distinct geographic regions of Africa?

2. How have conditions in the rainforest affected human activity in that region?

3. How did Kush's relations with Egypt change over the years?

4. How did Axum become a powerful city?

5. What set the eastern coast apart from other African kingdoms?

6. What two cultures blended to develop Swahili?

7. How did geographic conditions limit contact between Africans and people from outside of the Middle East?

8. Why was the gold-salt trade important to the development of West Africa?

9. What were Mansa Musa's most important achievements?

10. What caused the downfall of Songhai?

11. How did African religions embrace polytheism and monotheism?

12. What purposes did the arts serve in African society?

13. How did the lineage system ensure that society's values would be upheld?

14. What two geographic features dominate South America?

15. How do most scientists believe that the first people reached the Americas?

16. When and where did farming begin in the Americas?

17. What can be inferred about Mississippian society from the remains at Cahokia?

18. What characteristics did the Hopewell and Anasazi societies share?

19. How was the origin of civilization in Peru similar to that of the river valley civilizations of Egypt and Mesopotamia?

20. How were the Inca rulers able to maintain control over their vast empire?

21. What were three major achievements of Maya civilization?

22. Why did the Aztec sacrifice human beings to their gods?

23. Both the Aztec and the Inca created formidable empires. What weaknesses, if any, did these empires have?

Lesson 44: Aztec Notes

Location: Mexico, 1300-1600 A.D.

Capital: Tenochtitlan (present day Mexico City), also the largest city; originally built on an island in Lake Texcoco.

Achievements:
- Created floating gardens called "chinampas"
- Created the tax system: this made them very rich because after they conquered a region, that region would pay taxes.
- Had an army: this allowed them to conquer many regions
- Used irrigation to water crops
- Kept records using hieroglyphics
- Had doctors and created over 1,000 medicines using plants

Other notes about Aztecs:
- Warlike
- Religion very important
- Offered human sacrifices to the sun god
- Conquered by Cortes and the Spanish

(From GAVL, creative commons 3.0 [https://creativecommons.org/licenses/by/3.0/], http://cms.gavirtualschool.org/Shared/ SocialStudies/WorldHistory/ EarlyAfrMesoAmSocieties)

Lesson 44: Inca Notes

Location:
- Nearly the whole Inca Empire was part of the rugged Andes Mountain chain
- The pre-imperial homeland of the Incas was a small area along the Urubamba River Valley, or the eastern side of the Andes of present-day Peru
- The origins of the Incas are murky
- Archaeological evidence suggests they were a regional ethnic group, or tribe, living around present-day Cuzco. However, Inca oral tradition has them emerging from the chilly depths of the high Andes lake, Titicaca.

Organization:
- There may have been as many as eight Supreme Inca rulers before the greatest of the Incas, Pachacuti, claimed the throne around 1438
- The foundation of the Inca empire was their ability to grow excess food and store it
- The Incas' unique social organization brought together over 7 million people, speaking many different languages, and spanning over 2,000 miles
- All worked towards a common purpose
- The Incas had no written language

Accomplishments:
- Like nowhere else in the Americas, the people of the Andes had for over a thousand years domesticated beasts of burden: alpacas and llamas
- The Incas built stoneworks capable of withstanding tremendous earthquakes
- The Incas built 20,000 miles of roads
- The Incas achieved a great empire through a remarkable organization of human labor
- Human labor was the coin of the Inca Empire
- Through a system of communication called quipu, information was constantly flowing through the empire by runners
- The Incas created a world of magnificent accomplishment
- The Incas made pottery, including small effigies depicting animals such as llamas, alpacas, and the large predator of the region – the jaguar
- Utilitarian pots, beakers, and dual bottles with simple repetitive geometric patterns are distinctly Inca
- The Inca state organize artisan women to produce distinctive textiles
- The Incas are most famous for their spectacular stonework and naturalistic artistic design

Lesson 44: Inca Notes (cont.)

Machu Picchu:
- Machu Picchu, the temple palace in the clouds, is the crown jewel of Inca architecture and design
- Started by Pachacuti, but never completed, Machu Picchu was never touched, damaged, or looted by the Spanish
- Lost to the ages, Mach Picchu was rediscovered in 1911 by Hiram Bingham
- Machu Picchu is sharply divided into two parts: and agricultural area and an urban area

Lesson 45: Mesoamerican Societies Chart   World History

	Olmecs/ Mayans	Aztecs	Incas
Dates of Civilization			
Geographic Location			
Major Cities			
Description of Government			
Characteristics of Religion			
Description of Economy/Agriculture			
Significant Cultural Achievements			

Lesson 48: Dark Ages Notes

Causes of the Dark Ages:
- Barbarian invasion brought down the Roman Empire
- Roman Empire was already in decline militarily, economically, socially, politically

Absence of Civilization:
- 5 key traits of civilization
  - Writing
  - Advanced technology
  - Specialization of workers
  - Growth of cities
  - Complex institutions

- Writing and learning suffered
  - Barbarians destroyed much of existing literature
  - Christians strongly supported that the only acceptable literature was the Bible
    - As a result, almost all education took place in schools and monasteries

- Technology suffered
  - With absence of learning supported by lack of reading materials, few would have the knowledge required to make improvements
  - With most learning centered in the church, there was little interest in technological improvement

- Specialization of workers suffered
  - With the absence of large trading centers (cities), there was little need for specialization and strong need of self-sufficiency (many skills required)

- Growth of cities suffered
  - Barbarians destroyed many of the largest cities
  - Lack of government and trade meant there was little need to rebuild the cities

- Complex institutions suffered
  - Barbarians destroyed the existing government
  - Lack of large cities meant little need for larger organizations
  - Only significant institution left was the church
    - This led to the church gaining significant power throughout Europe

Lesson 48: Dark Ages Notes (cont.)

Government:

- Family ties and personal loyalty replace government as the force holding people together.
    - Warriors banded together in groups of 15-30
    - Pledged loyalty to one leader in each group
    - Lived under their leader's roof
- German kingdoms began to spring up throughout Europe
- German warriors would not follow unfamiliar kings. They would only be loyal to their clan leader.
- All of this combined to make larger government virtually impossible

Lesson 48: Power of the Church Notes

The Politics of Conversion:
- The Franks and the Church
  - Frankish rulers viewed themselves as protectors of the papacy
  - Charlemagne also worked to spread Christianity in northern lands

- The spread of Christianity
  - Charlemagne's military campaigns forced the Saxons to accept Christianity
  - Pagan ways did not disappear immediately
  - By 1000 AD, all of western Europe had adopted Roman Christianity

The Papacy:
- Pope Gregory I (590-604 AD)
  - Organized defense of Rome against the Lombard menace
  - Reasserted papal primacy over other bishops
  - Strongly emphasized the sacrament of penance

- The conversion of England
  - Gregory's missionary campaigns in western Europe
  - First converted English kings
  - By 800 AD, England was securely in the fold of the Roman church

Monasticism:
- Origin
  - Devout Christians practiced asceticism in deserts of Egypt in the 2nd and 3rd century
  - Monastic lifestyle became popular when Christianity became legal in the 4th century

- Monastic rules
  - St. Benedict (480-547 AD) provided a set of regulations
  - Virtues of Benedictine monks: poverty, chastity, and obedience

- St. Scholastica (482-543 AD)
  - St. Benedict's sister, a nun
  - Adapted the Rule and provided guidance for religious life of women

- Roles of monasteries
  - Became dominant feature in social and cultural life of western Europe
  - Accumulated large landholdings
  - Organized much of the rural labor force for agricultural production
  - Provided a variety of social services
    - Inns and shelters for travelers and refugees
    - Orphanages and medical centers
    - Schools
    - Libraries and scriptoria
  - Monks patiently and persistently served the needs of the rural population

Lesson 48: Feudal Society Notes

The Feudal System:
- Lords and vassals
  - Lord provided vassal a grant known as a benefice, usually grants of land often called fiefs
    - Enabled the vassal to devote time and energy to serve the lord
    - Provided resources to maintain horses and military equipment
  - Vassals owed the lord loyalty, obedience, respect, counsel, and military service
  - The lord-vassal relationship was not entirely new, but became dominant

- Feudal politics
  - Multi-tiered network of lord-vassal relationships
  - Political stability depended on discipline and control of vassals

Serfs and Manors in Feudal Europe:
- Serfs
  - Slaves and peasants took agricultural tasks, frequently intermarried
  - Free peasants often turned over themselves and their lands to a lord for protection
  - Serfs as an intermediate category emerged about the mid-7th century

- Serfs' obligations
  - Labor service and rents in kind
  - Could not move to other lands without permission
  - Obligations fulfilled, serfs had right to work on land and pass it to heirs

- Manors
  - Principle form of agricultural organization
  - A manor was a large estate controlled by the lord and his deputies
  - Many lords had the authority to execute serfs for serious misconduct
  - Manors were largely self-sufficient communities

(From GAVL, creative commons 3.0 [https://creativecommons.org/licenses/by/3.0/], http://cms.gavirtualschool.org/Shared SocialStudies/ WorldHistory/MidAges/FeudalSocietyReadingNotes.pdf)

Lesson 48: Developments of the Mid. Ages Notes World History

Agriculture:
- Agricultural production had suffered from repeated invasions during the Dark Ages
- Small wooden plows of Mediterranean farmers did not work well in the north

Heavy Plows:
- Heavy plows appeared in the 900s that could turn soil deeper and easier
- Became common by the 1000s, agricultural production increased
- Cultivation of new lands, watermills, and rotating crops

From a Rural Society to a More Urban Society:
- Agricultural production not enough to support large cities during the Dark Ages
- As food production increased and created surpluses, many people could now turn to other tasks, such as trading

Trade:
- Trade and urban centers began to develop by the 11th century as many of the crusading armies began returning with goods from the Middle East
- Trade took place in the Mediterranean, North Sea, and Black Sea

Population:
- In 200 AD, European population stood at 36 million
- In 400 AD, 31 million
- In 600 AD, 26 million
- In 800 AD, edged up to 29 million
- In 900 AD, 30 million
- By 1000 AD, back to 36 million

(From GAVL, creative commons 3.0 [https://creativecommons.org/licenses/by/3.0/], http://cms.gavirtualschool.org/Shared SocialStudies/ WorldHistory/MidAges/DevelopmentsHighMiddleAgesReadingNotes.pdf)

Lesson 58: Middle Ages Chart

Subject	Major Characteristics
Dark Ages	
Feudalism	
Crusades	
High Middle Ages	

(From GAVL, creative commons 3.0 [https://creativecommons.org/licenses/by/3.0/], http://cms.gavirtualschool.org/Shared/
SocialStudies/WorldHistory/MidAges/MiddlesAgesChart.pdf)

Lesson 62: Renaissance Notes

The Renaissance Period: 14th-17th Centuries

1. Renaissance means rebirth or revival – historical period of approximately 300 years marked by a revival in art, literature, and learning.

2. The Renaissance period served as a bridge or transition between **medieval** and **modern** Western Europe.

Distinctive Features:

1. It began with the rediscovery of **Greco-Roman Civilization** which had been neglected during the **Middle Ages**.

2. It emphasized reason, a questioning attitude, experimentation, and free inquiry.
   - This contrasted with the medieval concern with faith, authority, and tradition.

3. It glorified the individual and approved worldly pleasures, viewing life as worthwhile for its own sake, not chiefly as a preparation for the life to come (salvation).

4. Focused attention upon **secular society** rather than the medieval preoccupation with the Church and religious affairs.

5. Featured great achievements in literature, art, and science.

Origin of the Renaissance in Italy:

1. Italy had been the center of Greco-Roman Culture. It contained sculpture, buildings, roads, and manuscript that excited curiosity about **classical civilization**.

2. Located on the Mediterranean, Italy had absorbed stimulating new ideas from the more advanced **Byzantine and Moslem Worlds**.

3. Benefiting from the revival of trade that resulted from the Crusades, Italy had wealthy influential people who became **patrons** (supporters) of literature, art, and science.

Leading Patrons:

1. Certain Popes in Rome

2. The **Sforza** family in **Milan**

3. The **Medici** family in **Florence**

Florence: Preeminent Renaissance City:
1. 15th Century: Florence came under the control (rule) of the **Medici** family.
   - Originally a merchant family who amassed a fortune in the wool trade and then expanded into banking.
2. The Meidicis (especially **Lorenzo the Magnificent**, 1469-1492) became outstanding patrons of Renaissance Art.
3. Florence attracted people of talent from elsewhere in Italy, and the city acquired many priceless works of art.

The Renaissance Spreads:
1. In the 15th century, Renaissance ideas began to spread from Italy to France, the German states, Holland, and England.
2. The spread of these ideas resulted from religious, military, and commercial contacts.
3. Many northern scholars also traveled to Italy to absorb Italian art and learning.

Humanism – Illustrated the Spirit of the Renaissance (a literary movement that began in the 14th Century Italy)
1. Concerned themselves not with religious matters, but with everyday human problems.
2. Drew inspiration from classical civilization – eagerly seeking, studying, and publicizing ancient Greek and Roman manuscripts.
3. Revived interest, chiefly among educated people, in literature and writing.

Early Humanist Writers:
1. **Petrarch** (1304-1374)
   - Italian who studied the classics and wrote in both Italian and Latin
   - Imitated the style of classical writers.
2. Pico della **Mirandola** (1463-1494)
   - An Italian who lived for a while near Florence and was a scholar of law, philosophy, Greek, Latin, Hebrew, and Arabic.
   - He spoke in praise of the **dignity of human beings**.
3. **Erasmus** (1466?-1536)
   - He was Dutch and a brilliant classical scholar.

- In his book, *Praise of Folly*, he ridiculed superstition, prejudice, upper class privileges, and Church abuses.
- By satirizing social evils, Erasmus encouraged people to think about reforms.

4. **Sir Thomas More** (1478-1535)
   - An Englishman, he wrote *Utopia*, a book about an ideal country that was free from war, injustice, poverty, and ignorance.

The Vernacular Replaces Latin in Literature:

1. In the **Middle Ages**, Latin was the language of literature, of the Church, and of educated people.

2. Over the centuries, other languages had been evolving through **everyday usage**.

3. French, Italian, Spanish, German, and English are **vernacular** (national) languages.

4. At the end of the Middle Ages, writers began to use the vernacular instead of Latin.

Writers of the Vernacular:

1. **Dante** (1265-1321)
   - An Italian, born in Florence, who served that city in various governmental positions until he was exiled by political opponents.
   - Known as the **Father of Modern Italy**, he was the first to write an important piece of literature in the vernacular.
   - His *Divine Comedy* is a long poem in which he describes an imaginary trip through hell, purgatory, and heaven during which one of his guides is the Roman poet, **Virgil**.

2. **Boccaccio** (1313?-1375)
   - An Italian who lived in Florence during his formative years and was influenced by the Renaissance spirit of Humanism.
   - He is best known for his **Italian prose** in a collection of short stories called <u>The Decameron</u>.
     - These stories were related by a group of young men who fled to a villa outside Florence to escape the **Black Death** (plague).

3. **Chaucer** (1340?-1400)
   - An Englishman who became familiar with the works of Dante and Boccaccio while traveling in Italy.

- Chaucer used English in his collection of stories in verse, <u>The Canterbury Tales</u>.
  - Supposedly these stories were related by pilgrims journeying to the religious shrine at Canterbury.

The Invention of Printing – Encourages Literature:

1. During the Middle Ages books had to be hand copied (time-consuming and expensive) on parchment (goat skin).
2. 12th Century: Europeans discovered paper from the Moslems.
3. ca. 1450: printing with **movable type** was invented by a German, **Johan Gutenberg**.
4. Impact: printing tremendously increased output and accuracy and decreased the cost.
   - Inexpensive printed materials afforded all people opportunities for literacy and learning and encouraged talented people to write.

Renaissance Literary Achievements:

1. **Machiavelli** (1469-1527)
   - An Italian born in Florence who served the **Florentine Republic** as a secretary and diplomat.
   - When the Medici family was restored to power in Florence, Machiavelli was dismissed from office and permitted to retire to his country home where he devoted himself to writing.
   - *The Prince*: major work on ethics and government describing how rulers maintain power by methods that ignore right or wrong and accept the philosophy that "**the end justifies the means.**"
   - The word **Machiavellian** has come to mean "cunning and unscrupulous" – a prototype for a totalitarian dictator, right or left wing.

2. **Rabelais** (1494?-1553)
   - A Frenchman who wrote the romance *Gargantua and Panatagruel*.
   - A **humorist** who portrayed a comic world of giants whose adventures satirized education, politics, and philosophy.

3. **Montaigne** (1533-1592)
   - A Frenchman who wrote a series of essays.

- He expressed **skepticism** toward accepted beliefs, condemning superstition and intolerance and urging people to live nobly.
4. **Cervantes** (1547-1616)
   - A Spaniard who ridiculed feudal society, especially knighthood and chivalry, in relating the adventures of the mad knight of La Mancha, *Don Quixote*.

5. **Shakespeare** (1564-1616)
   - His plays employed a dramatic technique to probe historical events and human character.
   - Best known plays:
     - **Histories**: *Henry IV* and *Henry V*
     - **Comedies**: *Twelfth Night* and *Midsummer Night's Dream*
     - **Tragedies**: *Romeo and Juliet*, *Hamlet*, *Julius Caesar*, and *Macbeth*.

6. **Milton** (1608-1674)
   - Englishman
   - *Paradise Lost* – an epic poem that retold the Biblical story of creation and the Garden of Eden
   - *Areopagitica* – advocated freedom of the press.

7. **Moliere** (1622-1673)
   - Dominated French literature as its leading comic dramatist.
   - Best known plays: *The Misanthrope* and *The Imaginary Invalid*

Characteristics of Renaissance Art:

1. Influenced by the artistic achievements of **Classical Greece and Rome**, particularly in sculpture and architecture – Renaissance artists often imitated classical works.

2. Renaissance painting emphasized realism, attention to detail, and a desire for perfection.

3. **Early Renaissance** painters dealt with **religious themes** but with a lifelike approach.

4. **Later Renaissance** painters also employed a realistic style and continued to recreated Biblical themes. They also depicted worldly subjects, landscapes, portraits, and scenes of everyday life.

Italian Artistic Achievements of the Renaissance:

1. **Giotto** (1266?-1337)
   - A painter and architect born near Florence.

- Portrayed religious themes in many **frescos** (wall paintings); designed the Cathedral of Florence with its famous bell tower (known as Giotto's Tower)

2. **Ghiberti** (1378-1455)
   - A Florentine who sculpted a series of exquisite biblical scenes for the bronze doors of the baptistry in Florence.

3. **Donatello** (1386?-1466)
   - A Florentine sculptor best known for his life-size statue of St. George.

4. **Leonardo da Vinci** (1452-1519)
   - He worked in Florence, Milan, and Rome.
   - He was a skilled painter, sculptor, architect, musician, engineer, and scientist.
   - In military engineering, he improved the method of loading cannons and devised equipment for scaling walls.
   - He devised the possibility of a parachute and a flying machine
   - In painting, he is best known for his Self Portrait, The Last Supper, and the Mona Lisa

5. **Michelangelo** (1475-1564)
   - He worked in Florence and Rome; was talented as a painter, sculptor, poet, and architect.
   - Famed for the biblical scenes he painted on the ceiling of the Sistine Chapel in the Vatican.
   - As a sculptor, he is best known for his Pieta, David, and Moses
   - He also designed the dome of St. Peter's Basilica in Rome.

6. **Titian** (1477-1576)
   - A painter associated with Venice and known for his portrait of famous people and his scenes from mythology and the Bible, such as the Assumption of the Virgin.

7. **Raphael** (1483-1520)
   - Worked in both Florence and Rome
   - Known for the frescos he painted in the Papal Library at Rome.

Spanish Artistic Achievements of the Renaissance:
1. **El Greco** (1547-1614)
   - A Greek who settled in Spain, painted religious scenes such as the Assumption, portraits of church officials, and the famous landscape, View of Toledo.

2. **Velasquez** (1599-1660)

- Official painter to the court of King Philip IV of Spain; also did many paintings of royalty.
- Commemorated a Spanish victory against the Dutch in his Surrender of Breda.

Dutch Artistic Achievements of the Renaissance:

1. **Hals** (1580-1666)
   - Painted portraits of ordinary people and scenes of everyday life. He is famous for his Laughing Cavalier.

2. **Rembrandt** (1606-1669)
   - Considered the greatest painter of Northern Europe.
   - Portrayed everyday life and common people in his paintings.
   - Notable works: The Night Watch, The Anatomy Lesson, and Aristotle Contemplating the Bust of Homer.

Flemish Artistic Achievements of the Renaissance:

1. **Rubens** (1577-1640)
   - Depicted action in religious and historical paintings. Most famous for The Adoration of the Magi.

(Adapted from GAVL, creative commons 3.0 [https://creativecommons.org/licenses/by/3.0/], https://cms.gavirtualschool.org/Shared/SocialStudies/WorldHistory/RenRef/RenaissanceReadingNotes.pdf)

Lesson 67: Artist and Writer Chart

World History

Artist/Writer	Biography	Major works and years created
Michelangelo		
Leonardo da Vinci		
Raphael		
Erasmus		
Dante		
Petrarch		

Lesson 68: Protestant Reformation Notes

What Was the Reformation?
- The Reformation was a religious crisis within the Catholic Church where many people began to demand reforms or changes. People were unhappy with many aspects of the Church, so they either demanded change or broke off and created their own branches of the Christian faith.

Member Complaints Within the Catholic Church:
1. Many priests and popes were too concerned with worldly things to focus on their spiritual duties. Instead of focusing on being spiritual influences on Christians, they focused on studying the arts and ancient manuscripts – this left little time for them to do their jobs.

2. Lower clergy were very poorly educated (many couldn't even read) so they couldn't teach Scripture because they couldn't read the Bible.

3. Many clergy members did not follow the teachings of Scripture – they lived with women without being married, had children with many different women, etc.

4. The Church began selling **indulgences** – pardons from sin. If you committed a sin, you paid the Church money and you were sold forgiveness.

5. Church ceremonies were very focused on "pomp and circumstance" rather than spirituality.

The First Leaders of the Reformation:
1. **Erasmus**: from Holland – he criticized the lack of education among the clergy.

2. **Thomas More**: wrote *Utopia* where he criticized the Church's leadership and outlined his perfect society. He said that a perfect society should be based on mercy and reason, not on greed and corruption.

3. **Martin Luther**: a monk in Wittenberg – he was deeply offended by the actions of the clergy and the selling of indulgences. He wrote the *95 Theses* that outlined his complaints. He nailed them to the Church doors in Wittenberg so that all Church members could read them.

The Printing Press:
- The printing press helped the Reformation grow very quickly. Up until the invention of the printing press, books were copied by hand. Therefore, most people did not have access to books and writings

because there simply weren't many copies. When the printing press was invented, it meant that books and writings could be copied quickly and distributed to many people. So, the writings of Erasmus, More, and Luther began to be copied and distributed to people throughout Europe. This spread their ideas. The Bible was also copied. This allowed people to read Scripture for themselves and to see that the Church was not teaching or following the Bible. All of these changes caused people to demand reform.

Martin Luther: Martin Luther began having his teachings printed and this infuriated the Pope and the leaders of the Catholic Church. Luther taught the following three ideas:

1. Faith in God was the only way to earn salvation.
   - This contradicted the Church's teaching that you could buy indulgences for sins and still be saved.

2. The Bible is the sole authority for Christians to follow.
   - This threatened the power of the Pope

3. All Christians were equal.
   - This diminished the power of Church officials.

Luther's ideas began to spread, and the Catholic Church asked Charles V for help. Charles V was the Holy Roman Emperor and he had much power throughout Europe. He called Luther a heretic and an outlaw at the Diet of Worms and called for his execution. Christians throughout Europe began to leave the Catholic Church and to follow Luthe – they became known as Protestants. Luther died in 1546.

Henry VIII: Henry VIII became king of England in 1509. He needed a son to succeed him when he died. He and his wife never had a son who lived past infancy, so Henry asked the Pope to declare his marriage illegal. This way he could marry a new woman and hopefully have a son. The Pope refused Henry's request. Parliament allowed Henry a divorce and legalized his marriage to Anne Boleyn. Then they passed the Act of Supremacy which stated that the king was the head of the Christian Church in England. Henry created the Church of England which followed the same teachings as the Catholic Church EXCEPT that it allowed divore.

John Calvin: Calvin spread the teachings of Martin Luther to Switzerland. However, Calvin did change a few of Luther's ideas. Calvin taught that men and women were naturally evil and that there were only a select few who could be saved from sin. These people were called the **elect**. God, Calvin believed, was all-knowing and knew before people were born who would be saved and who would not, an idea called **predestination**. Calvin also taught that the "elect" should rule society and try to keep men and women from being sinful. Therefore, Calvin set up a theocracy in Switzerland, a government run by the Church.

John Knox: Knox spread Calvin's ideas to Scotland and his religion became known as Presbyterianism.

Huguenots: The followers of Cavlin and Luther in France were called Huguenots.

The Catholic Church Responds with the Counter-Reformation: The following three changes were called the Counter-Reformation because they were meant to stop the spread of Protestant Faiths.

1. In Spain, a group of devout Catholics joined together to defend Catholicism and the Pope. They were called **Jesuits** and they were often referred to as a spiritual "army." The Jesuits had three goals:
    1. to set up schools to teach Catholicism
    2. to spread Catholicism to other parts of the world
    3. to stop the Protestant faiths from spreading

2. The Council of Trent met in 1545: bishops, cardinals, and the Pope met in the town of Trent and decided that:
    1. The Pope's interpretation of the Bible was final
    2. Christians were saved by faith AND good works
    3. The Bible AND Church tradition should equally guide a Christian's life
    4. The selling of indulgences would be banned

3. Index of Forbidden Books was created. This was a list of books critical of the Catholic Church that were burned and banned in all Catholic cities.

Lesson 79: Reasons for Exploration Notes World History

Reasons for Exploration: Many European countries began to explore other parts of the world during the 1400s and 1500s. The reasons for this exploration were:

1. Many countries were searching for new spices to trade for. Spices were considered a luxury item and could be sold for high prices so merchants wanted them to sell.

2. Many people were trying to spread Christianity to parts of the world where Christianity was not accepted or heard of.

3. New technology such as compasses, maps, etc. made travel easier.

4. Kings and queens sent explorers in search of wealth to claim as their own.

5. Kings and queens wanted new lands where they could send criminals and anyone not welcome in their homelands.

(Adapted from GAVL, creative commons 3.0 [https://creativecommons.org/licenses/by/3.0/], https://cms.gavirtualschool.org/Shared/SocialStudies/WorldHistory/AgeofExploration/ReasonsForExplorationReadingNotes..pdf)

Lesson 79: Explorers Chart

Explorer	Sponsor Country	Reason for Exploration (Goals)	Part of the World Explored	Discoveries and Accomplishments
Prince Henry				
Bartholomeu Dias				
Vasco de Gama				
Christopher Columbus				
Amerigo Vespucci				
Vasco Nunez de Balboa				
Ferdinand Magellan				
Samuel de Champlain				
Robert La Salle				

Lesson 91: Enlightenment and Revolutions Terms World History

1. **Charles I** – King of England; executed by Oliver Cromwell

2. **Charles II** – Restored as King of England in 1646

3. **Cavaliers** – group that supported Charles I in English Revolution

4. **Roundheads** – group that supported Parliament and Cromwell in English revolution

5. **Puritans** – religious group that opposed King Charles I

6. **Oliver Cromwell** – leader of Parliament and the Roundheads; made dictator of England

7. **Glorious Revolution** – bloodless installment of William and Mary as monarchs of England

8. **William and Mary** – became monarchs of England in 1688

9. **John Locke** – English Enlightened philosopher; developed Social Contract theory of Government

10. **Thomas Hobbes** – English Enlightened philosopher; believed in a strong central government

11. **Leviathan** – book written by Thomas Hobbes

12. **Two Treaties on Government** – book by John Locke on government structure

13. **Divine Right of Kings** – belief by absolute monarchs that God had chosen them to rule

14. **Absolute Rulers** – monarchs that had total authority in their countries

15. **English Bill of Rights** – signed by William and Mary; gave Parliament ultimate control in England

16. **Philosophe** – Enlightenment philosophers in France

17. **Enlightenment** – movement begun n France; logic and reason could solve societal problems

18. **Isaac Newton** – Enlightened scientist; developed theory and laws of gravity

19. **Denis Dedirot** – wrote the first Encyclopedia

20. **Thomas Jefferson** – American founding father; wrote the Declaration of Independence

21. **Jean Jacques Rousseau** – Enlightened philosopher who preached on the separation of powers

22. **Adam Smith** – developed the idea of "laissez-faire" economics

23. **Voltaire** – French Enlightened philosophe; often criticized the Catholic Church

24. **Adam Montesquieu** – Enlightened philsophe who preached three branches of government

25. **Louis XVI** – absolute ruler of France in the early 1600's; the "Sun" King

26. **Old Regime** – social structure in France before 1789; made up of three estates

27. **Robespierre** – leader of the Reign of Terror phase of the French Revoluation

28. **Reign of Terror** – murderous phase of the French Revolution in 1793

29. **Napoleon Bonparte** – became emperor of France in 1804

30. **Marie Antoinette** – queen of France at the time of the French Revolution

31. **Great Fear** – wave of panic that swept the French peasants during the French Revolution

32. **Waterloo** – place in Belgium that was Napoleon's final defeat

33. **Continental System** – disastrous economic policy of Napoleon

34. **Bastille** – French armory; rebellion here began the French Revolution

35. **Peninsulares** – upper class in Latin American society; people born in Spain

36. **Creoles** – sons and daughters born in Latin American of the Peninsulares

37. **Mestizos** – people of Spanish and Latin American Indian descent

38. **Caudillo** – Latin American military dictators

39. **Toussaint L'Ouverture** – leader of the Haitian Revolution

40. **Bolivar** – leader of the revolution in Columbia

41. **San Martin** – leader of the revolution in Argentina

42. **Dom Pedro** – Mexican Revolutionary leader

43. **Hidalgo** – priest who helped begin the revolution in Mexico

44. **Taiping Rebellion** – (1850-64) Large scale rebellion against the Qing dynasty and the presence of foreigners in China

45. **Opium War** – war between Britain and China in the 1800's

46. **Commodore Matthew Perry** – Commodore of the U.S. Navy who compelled the opening of Japan to the West with the Convention of Kanagawa in 1854

47. **Tokugawa Teyasu** – Shogun of Japan in the 1600's

Lesson 91: Enlightenment Thinkers Chart

Person	Country/Title	Dates Lived	Interesting Fact	Major Accomplishment
Tokugawa Ieyasu				
Peter the Great				
Louis XIV				
Phillip II				
Jean-Jacques Rousseau				
Voltaire				
John Locke				
John Locke				
Thomas Hobbes				

Lesson 91: Enlightenment Thinkers Chart

World History

Person	Country/Title	Dates Lived	Interesting Fact	Major Accomplishment
Isaac Newton				
Copernicus				
Galileo				
Thomas Jefferson				
Montesquieu				

Lesson 95: The Age of Absolute Monarchs Notes World History

The Age of Absolute Monarchs: During the period of absolute monarchs (1500-1763), many changes took place throughout Europe. Individual countries were developing and experiencing many conflicts – the biggest of which was between Protestants and Catholics. These notes give you a general overview of the time period and the events taking place.

Spain

By 1500, Spain was very wealthy due to the gold and silver they were collecting from their colonies abroad.

Philip II became the ruler of Spain in 1556. His two main goals were to strengthen his own power and to spread Catholicism throughout Spain. Philip's two main rivals were the Netherlands (a colony of Spain) and England because both places were strongly Protestant. In 1558, Philip sent his Armada (navy) to attack England and try to conquer it to make it a Catholic country under Spanish control. His attack was foiled and the Armada was defeated. Then, in 1581 the Netherlands revolted against Spain and won their independence. Both of these defeats were crushing blows to Spain.

Netherlands

The Netherlands gained their independence from Spain in 1581. The Dutch living in the Netherlands were unique because they practiced religious toleration and allowed all religions to be practiced openly and freely. The Dutch were also unique because they were very innovative in terms of their economy:

- The Dutch were the first to use capitalism. Capitalists were people who invested large sums of money into businesses. They hoped to pay all of the costs of running the business PLUS make a profit. The profit was then re-invested into new businesses. As a result, businesses flourished in the Netherlands and they became one of the largest traders in all of Europe.

- The Dutch also ran a very successful banking system. People from all over Europe deposited their money into Dutch banks. This made the Dutch very rich because they were able to loan some of this money out and charge interest on the loans.

- The Dutch East Indies Company was founded in 1602. This allowed many businessmen to invest in a trading company. The traders would go to Asia and the Caribbean to get spices which they would then take back to the Netherlands and sell. This made the investors in the Dutch East Indies Company very rich!

France

In 1559, Catherine de Medici became the ruler of France (when her husband died). At this time, France was deeply divided over religious conflict between Protestants and Catholics. The majority of France's population was Catholic but Protestants were growing in number. The St. Bartholomew's Day Massacre only made the conflict between the two groups worse. Catholic mobs hunted down Protestants and murdered them – over 12,000 Huguenots were killed. Catherine was blamed for allowing this to happen (since she was Catholic and didn't try to stop the killings). Catherine ruled until her death and France stayed in religious conflict.

Henry IV took power of France in 1589. He was a member of the Bourbon family and he was Protestant – this created much conflict with Catholics. As a result, Henry became Catholic. However, he wanted to keep the Huguenots happy as well, so he allowed Huguenots to worship openly and freely in France. This was declared in the Edict of Nantes. He ruled until his death in 1610.

Louis XIII became king when his father, Henry IV, died in 1610. He was not a competent ruler so he turned most of his power over to one of his advisors, Cardinal Richelieu. He revoked many of the Huguenots' rights.

When Louis XIII died, his son, Louis XIV, became king of France. He ruled very lavishly and lived grandly (that's why he was called the Sun King). He partied and built an amazing palace called Versailles.

Louis wanted France to be the most powerful country in Europe so he turned a lot of his power over to his financial advisor, Colbert. Colbert believed in mercantilism or the idea that a country needed to export (selling goods to foreign countries) than it needed to import (buying goods from foreign countries). Colbert gave subsidies or tax benefits to French companies which encouraged them to grow and expand. He also placed high tariffs (taxes) on imported goods – this made them very expensive so most people couldn't afford them. All of this helped France's economy to grow and become prosperous.

Louis made two tragic mistakes, however, which caused him great conflict with his own people. First, Louis revoked the Edict of Nantes which meant that Huguenots could no longer freely practice their religion – this rekindled the fighting between Catholics and Protestants in France. Second, Louis tried to capture the throne of Spain in 1700. This began the War of Spanish Succession which was very costly for France. This war almost bankrupted France and left many people suffering.

Germany (then called the Holy Roman Empire):

In 1555, the princes in Germany (then called the Holy Roman Empire) agreed that churches in Germany could be Catholic or Lutheran (but not Calvinist – they didn't want a theocracy so Calvinism was banned). This was all agreed upon in the Peace of Augsburg. By 1618, however, Protestants and Catholics were fighting for control of the empire in the Thirty Years' War.

Ferdinand II became emperor of the Holy Roman Empire in 1619. He was a member of the Hapsburg family and he was Catholic. He began trying to force the entire empire to become Catholic. From 1618 to 1630, the Hapsburg army destroyed Protestant villages throughout the empire. By 1630, however, the Protestants began to receive financial aid from outside countries and they were able to fight back. The war raged on until 1648. In 1648, the Treaty of Westphalia was signed and ended the Thirty Years' War. The Treaty divided up the Holy Roman Empire into independent countries.

England

In 1558, Elizabeth I became queen of England. She was a member of the Tudor family and she faced religious conflict within her country. To resolve the conflict, Elizabeth had Parliament pass the Act of Uniformity and the Act of Supremacy. The Act of Uniformity created one legal church in England – the Church of England. The sermons were delivered in English, not Latin (made the Protestants happy) but the services were still very lavish and formal (made the Catholics happy). The Act of Supremacy made Elizabeth the head of the Church of England.

In 1567, devout Catholics became unhappy with Elizabeth's compromises between Catholicism and Protestantism. They encouraged Elizabeth's cousin, Mary Stuart, Queen of Scots, to try and dethrone Elizabeth. She went to

England and lived with Elizabeth. Elizabeth discovered her plot to dethrone her and she had Mary beheaded.

In 1588, Spain attacked England. Philip II wanted to conquer England and make it completely Catholic. Elizabeth sent Francis Drake and his Sea Dogs (navy) to fight the Spanish and they defeated them.

Russia

In 1613, the Romanovs came to power in Russia. Russia was isolated from the rest of the world and the majority of the population was very poor. Czar Peter I dreamed of modernizing Russia. He traveled throughout Europe in secret looking at how European cities were organized and how the people lived. When he returned to Russia he made many changes. Women were encouraged to attend social gatherings and no longer had to wear veils. The European/ Christian calendar was adopted. Farmers were taught how to grow potatoes and new crops. Peter built many factories and he encouraged exporting. He also encouraged the mining of iron ore so that Russia could sell iron to foreign countries and make money. Last, he began the first newspaper in Russia so that Russian citizens could know what was going on in their own country and around the world. Peter then moved the capital of Russia to St. Petersburg.

Austria

After the end of the Thirty Years' War, Austria became an independent region. It was ruled by the Hapsburgs. Maria Theresa spent many years as queen and fought many wars to defend Austria against Prussian attacks.

Prussia

The Hohenzollerns ruled Prussia when it became independent after the Holy Roman Empire was divided. The focused much of their attention on building their military and often went to war with Austria trying to gain more territory.

(Adapted from GAVL, creative commons 3.0 [https://creativecommons.org/licenses/by/3.0/], https://cms.gavirtualschool.org/Shared/ SocialStudies/WorldHistory/AgeEnlightAgeRev/AgeofAbsoluteMonarchs.pdf)

Lesson 95: French Revolution Notes

French Monarchy faces a crisis:

Old Regime has three estates:

1. First Estate
   - Roman Catholic Church and the clergy, making up 10%
   - Did not pay taxes, although incredibly wealthy

2. Second Estate
   - They held the highest positions in government, courts, army
   - Nobles owning 20% of land, made up less than 2% population
   - Paid no taxes and refused to pay them

3. Third Estate – 98% of the population
   - **Bourgeoisie**
     - City-dwelling middle class, many educated, treated like peasants
     - Called the culottes for the types of clothes
   - **Urban lower class**
     - Workers of cities (butchers, tailors, weavers, etc.)
     - Called the sans-culottes
   - **Peasant farmers**
     - Largest group, made up 4/5 of population
     - Lost ½ of income to taxes and had to pay taxes in the form of work

Louis XVI was a weak ruler

1. Married to the hated Marie Antoinette
2. In debt because of involvement in the Seven Years War (French and Indian War)
3. Tried to tax nobles, but nobles required a call of the Estates General

National Assembly takes power

1. National Assembly was actually the Third Estate
2. Third Estate clamors for power – the First and Second Estates always overruled them
3. They decide to end the monarchy, the first act of revolution

Storming of the Bastille (a prison)

1. The National Assembly wanted to get inside Bastille because of the supply of gunpowder

2. Needed it to defend themselves against Swiss troops marching in to break up riots

3. The storming was important because it reduced the king's power and saved the National Assembly

4. The day commemorating it is similar to July 4th in the United States

Great Fear sweeps France

1. The group of Parisian women eventually stormed the queen's apartment

2. This caused King Louis XVI to go to Paris

3. Revolution leads to reform August 4, 1789; people continue to speak about revolution

Assembly adopts many reforms

1. The new slogan of the revolution became "Liberty, Equality, Fraternity"

2. Rights of Man – "men are born and remain free and equal in rights"

3. A Declaration of the Rights of Man and of the Citizen written

4. Limited Monarchy – form of government similar to Britain

5. Departments – 83 districts each with elected local ruler

6. State-controlled church

- Eventually caused a split between the peasants and bourgeoisie, leading the peasants to resist revolution
- King Louis XVI tried to escape, but was found on the Netherlands' border, he lost all credibility

Three factions split France

1. The radicals who advocated change (left side of the hall)

2. The conservatives who believed that the King was the way to go (right side of the hall)

3. The centrists held the middle ground (sat in the middle)

France goes to war with Austria

1. The ruler of Austria was Marie Antoinette's brother

2. In 1792, the Austrian army was winning until he threatened war if the royal family was harmed

3. The new governing body was named National Convention

The Radicals execute Louis XVI

1. Radicals are people that continually want more and more change
2. The radicals abolished the monarchy and allowed France to become a republic
3. Eventually, Louis was found to be a common citizen, condemned to death, and beheaded by the guillotine

France creates a citizen-army

1. The First Coalition included Britain, Spain, Portugal, Prussia, and Austria
2. Although outnumbered, the dedicated French patriots were victorious

Robespierre ("The Incorruptible") began the Terror

1. Many peasants were afraid of the constant beheadings of church and governmental leaders
   - Maximilien Robespierre eventually came to power
2. Two changes to the calendar include making every month have 30 days and changing the name to make more sense
   - Robespierre formed the Committee of Public Safety in 1793
3. Many leaders and radicals were eventually beheaded because they were judged to be an enemy of the republic
4. Many historians believe over 40,000 were killed, nearly 80% were of the Third Estate, supposedly who the revolution was supposed to help

Robespierre falls from power

- He fell from power because of the paranoia surrounding him

Moderates rule in the Directory

1. New government switches to the right (less radical)
2. They find a conservative general named Napoleon making his headways

Napoleon rose through the army

- At the age of 16, joins the army
- October of 1795 guards the palace of the National Convention
- He is put in charge of attacking Austria through the Alps – marches into Milan and makes Italy a republic ruled by France

Napoleon seized power in France

- He seizes power because of the distrust of the people towards the new government
- He then sends 500 of his troops into the chamber to occupy it
- They form a consul (3 rulers) with him being one; this completes the coup

Second Coalition attacked France

- Constant war and English attacks against shipping lead Napoleon to fight
- Second Coalition includes Russia, Britain, and Austria against France
- Again Napoleon marches over Alps and forces Austria and Russia to surrender
- Britain and France sign the Treaty of Amiens in 1802 and there is 10 years of peace in Europe

Napoleon became emperor

- Napoleon plays the role of leader well
- A plebiscite (yes or no) vote by people ratifies the constitution which essentially gives all the power to one consul (Napoleon)
- In 1802, another vote makes him consol for life
- In 1804, another vote makes him emperor, crown goes from Pope to him

Napoleon restored order

- Economic order – stopped inflation and set up national bank
- Social order – nobles welcomed back, promotions based on merit
- Religious order – recognized Catholic as "the great majority of Frenchman;" also allowed people to worship how they pleased
- Legal order:
    a. Napoleonic Codes granted equal rights to all (ending the Three Estates)

b. Gave Napoleon ability to censor newspapers
c. Reinstated slavery in Caribbean colonies
d. Many women lost the rights they had gained through the revolution

Napoleon extended France's power

Napoleon dominated Europe

Napoleon's decline begins

- National set up the Continental System

- Guerrillas fought the French in Spain

- Napoleon invaded Russia

- A coalition defeated Napoleon and he was exiled to Elba, an island in the Mediterranean Sea

- Napoleon returned briefly but was defeated at a final battle in Waterloo, Belgium

- He was again exiled, this time on the isolated island in the Atlantic, St. Helena.

- He died in St. Helena in 1521

The Consolidation of Latin America, 1830-1920

European imperialism in the nineteenth century swallowed up much of Southeast Asia, India, Africa, and the Pacific. Three areas escaped full inclusion in the imperialist net: East Asia, Russia, and the Middle East. More surprisingly, Latin America, one of the earliest European colonial ventures, successfully cast off European political control and gained independence.

Latin American political leaders were shaped in the era of Enlightenment beliefs and accepted concepts common in the West, such as progress and rights in property. Despite some common ideology, the new nations faced numerous problems inherited from their colonial past.

From Colonies to Nations

By the late eighteenth century, Creole elites in Latin America were prepared to separate from Spain, but fear of racial and class conflict prevented successful action. Revolution occurred only after the Napoleonic wards disrupted the government of Spain.

The revolutions in Latin America were part of a series of rebellions from the American Revolution through the French Revolution. In 1791, slaves under Toussaint L'Overture successfully overthrew the colonial government of St. Domingue and established the independent republic of Haiti. The more radical aspects of the French Revolution and the specter of black rebellion in Haiti frightened the Creole elites of Latin America. What precipitated rebellion was the breakdown of the Spanish monarchy during the Napoleonic wars. In Latin America, Creoles set up independent governments that claimed to rule in the name of the exiled Spanish monarch.

Rebellion in Mexico began in 1810 under the leadership of Father Miguel de Hidalgo, who called on the support of mestizos and Indians. Hidalgo's movement failed for lack of Creole support, but a second revolutionary movement with more Creole support broke out in 1820. Under a Creole military officer, Augustin de Iturbide, the revolutionaries seized Mexico City and proclaimed Iturbide emperor in 1821. Mexico initially maintained control over Central America but separated from its southern neighbors in 1838. In northern South America, Simon Bolivar emerged as the leader of the revolutionary forces. Between 1817 and 1822 he defeated Spanish forces in Venezuela, Colombia, and Ecuador to form the new nation of Gran Colombia.

After 1830, these nations split into independent states. In southern South America, the revolutionary leader was Jose de San Martin. An Argentinean, San Martin mobilized resistance in his native colony, then crossed the Andes to Chile. By 1824, San Martin had carried the revolution into the most conservative colony of Peru and defeated the Spanish forces there. All of Spanish South America had won independence by 1825.

Independence in Brazil was achieved by different methods. Early movements for independence failed because of the general fear of slave uprisings. In 1807, the entire Portuguese royal family fled their home country in the face of a French invasion and emigrated to Brazil, where a government in exile was set up. The Portuguese king, Dom John VI, ruled his empire from Rio de Janeiro. Brazilian ports were opened to international commerce. When the king returned to Portugal in 1820, his son proclaimed independence in Brazil in 1822. Brazil became a monarchy under Dom Pedro I.

New Nations Confront Old and New Problems

Most of the independent nations accepted the need to establish representative governments, rights to private property, and free trade. There was less agreement over the position of the Roman Catholic Church in the new states. Revolutionary ideals led to the abolition of slavery in all states except Brazil and the remaining Spanish colonies. Voting rights tended to be restricted by race to favor Creoles, and women remained without voting rights. Indian populations and people of mixed origins remained outside the egalitarian principles of the new governments.

Mexico quickly abandoned its experiment with monarchy and established a republic in 1832. Its government remained unstable until the 1860s. In Central America, initial attempts to form a unified government gave way to individual states in 1838. Cuba and Puerto Rico remained within the orbit of Spanish colonialism. Consolidation also failed in South America. New Granada, Bolivar's attempt to unify northern South America, failed in 1830. The attempts of Rio de la Plata to transform revolutionary leadership into a political union failed. Paraguay, Uruguay, and Chile remained independent. Peru and Bolivia temporarily united, but they formed separate governments in 1839. Poor transportation and communication networks magnified problems of national integration.

Decades of war gave rise to regional military figures, or caudillos, who dominated local areas and sometimes seized national governments. Caudillos often operated out of self-interest, but they were capable of seeking support from regional elites or from Indians, peasants, or the poor.

Disagreements arose within the new governments over the degree of centralization the new republican governments should have. Federalists wished regional governments to establish policies, while centrists wanted powerful, central administrations. Liberals tended to support federalist policies, while political conservatives wanted centralized governments and supported corporate institutions, such as the Catholic Church. Liberals attempted to limit the role of the Church in civil affairs. Political parties representing these points of view sprang up in many of the new republics. Regardless of political view, leaders in Latin America tended to come from the class of wealthy landowners. Rapid political change was the rule in Latin America in the first half century after independence. Constitutions and leadership came and went swiftly. Brazil, with its monarchy, was perhaps the most stable government in the region.

Latin American Economies and World Markets, 1820-1870

Great Britain's determination to recognize Latin American independence forestalled European plans to restore the Spanish empire. The United States also supported the independence movement through the Monroe Doctrine of 1823. Britain's support for the new nations was tied to the opening of trade with Latin America. Britain rapidly replaced Spain as the region's largest trading partner. The dominance of the British hindered the development of Latin American industries and reinforced the economic dependence of Latin America in the world trade network.

From 1820 to 1850, the post-independence economy of Latin America remained stagnant. After 1850, in response to European demand for Latin American products, the economy quickened.

Enhanced trade permitted greater state development of important infrastructure, such as roads and railroads. The pattern was established that the Latin American economy was strictly dependent on levels of imports supported through the world trade network. Uneasy alliances between peasants and conservatives prevented rapid economic change proposed by the urban middle class.

In the last quarter of the nineteenth century, another surge in the European economy produced greater demand for Latin American products. Economies expanded rapidly. The economic growth created support for liberal policies and led to liberal governments after 1860. Attempts to impose European economic models on Latin American economies often failed. Immigrants from Europe entered Latin America to fill a labor demand that ignored Indian populations. Wealthy landowners continued to monopolize the countryside at the expense of small farmers.

The federalist constitution of 1824 failed to address the inequitable distribution of land or the status of the Indian population of Mexico. It was quickly abandoned in favor of military leadership. For much of the period after 1835, Antonio Lopez de Santa Anna served as the most important military and political figure in Mexico. Santa Anna enjoyed mixed results in fighting off foreign attempts to intervene in Mexico. Anglo-American settlers in the northern province of Texas rebelled and declared independence. Failure to suppress the Texas independence movement led to the United States' annexation of the region in 1845. The United States won the Mexican-American War and forced the cession of Texas, California, and much of Mexico's territory north of the Rio Grande River.

Mexico's failures in foreign policy at last led to the removal of Santa Anna as the chief political figure of the republic. Liberal rebellion against the caudillo resulted in Santa Anna's ouster and the creation of a liberal constitution. Conservatives rejected the liberal constitution and turned to France as an ally. French forces overthrew the republic and placed Maximilian von Habsburg on the throne as emperor in 1862. When French forces were withdrawn, liberals returned to power under Benito Juarez in 1867. Juarez continued to govern until his death in 1872.

In Brazil, a functioning republic existed behind the façade of monarchy. Independence was achieved in 1822 under Dom Pedro I, who ruled as king. When Dom Pedro I was deposed in 1831, a series of regencies ruled in the name of the young Dom Pedro II. Between 1831 and 1840, regional governments opposed centralized rule from Rio de Janeiro. After 1840, Dom Pedro II ruled in his own name as a liberal who sought to increase economic growth. The Brazilian economy was revolutionized by the emergence of coffee as an export crop.

As coffee production expanded, slavery was intensified as a source of coercive labor. As with other liberal governments of the period, Dom Pedro II improved the country's infrastructure and sought foreign investments to capitalize internal projects. Extensive European immigration into Brazil broadened the labor force and reduced the need for slavery. In 1888, slavery was finally abolished. Weakened by long participation in an unpopular war and by opposition from the Church, the monarchy did not long survive the abolition of slavery. In 1889, a military coup deposed the emperor and established a republic.

Conclusion: New Nations, Old Problems

During the nineteenth century, the former colonies of Latin America constructed new nations. There were many difficulties. Latin America was forced to forge economies in a world trade network already dominated by European nations. The new nations carried with them colonial social systems that were strictly hierarchical and in which a small Creole elite dominated the economy and politics. Indians, former slaves, and peasants shared little in the economic expansion of the second half of the century. In a sense, Latin America was the first region of the world to undergo the problems of decolonization.

(Adapted from GAVL, creative commons 3.0 [https://creativecommons.org/licenses/by/3.0/], https://cms.gavirtualschool.org/Shared/SocialStudies/WorldHistory/AgeEnlightAgeRev/LatinAmericanRevolutionsReadingNotes.pdf)

English Civil War

1. Describe 3 mistakes that Charles I made that led to the English Civil War.

2. What two sides fought the war? Which side supported Charles and which side did not? Which side was Catholic and which side was Protestant?

3. Who was Oliver Cromwell?

4. Who took control of England after Cromwell was removed?

5. Why is this significant in English history?

The American Revolution

1. Why did Britain begin interfering in the colonies' affairs in 1763?

2. What was the effect of the Stamp Act on the colonists?

3. What were the Townshend Acts and the colonists' response to them?

4. What was the Boston Massacre?

5. When did the First Continental Congress meet? What happened before they could meet?

6. Who was chosen as head of the Continental forces?

7. List three significant events during the war.

8. What was a lasting effect of the American Revolution?

The French Revolution and Napoleon

1. Why was the third estate unhappy with the old rules of voting?

2. What event marks the symbolic beginning of the French Revolution?

3. What changes did the National Assembly make in the French government?

4. Who were the king and queen of France when the revolution broke out? What happened to them?

5. Who was Maximillian Robespierre?

6. What was the "Reign of Terror"? When did it end?

7. When did Napoleon come to power?

8. What was the "Continental System" and why did it hurt the European continent economically?

9. What were some of the laws included in the "Napoleonic Code"?

10. What was Napoleon's biggest mistake in 1812?

11. Where was Napoleon's final defeat in 1815?

Latin American Questions

1. Who led the overthrow of the colonial government in St. Domingue in 1791?

2. When did the rebellion in Mexico begin?

3. Who defeated Spanish forces in Venezuela, Colombia, and Ecuador between 1817 and 1822?

4. Who was Jose de San Martin?

5. How did Brazil gain its independence?

6. What is the difference between Federalists and Centrists?

7. In what document did the United States support the independence of Latin America in 1823?

Lesson 101: China and Japan Reading Notes World History

Imperialism in China

China was not interested in trade with the outside world because they were totally self-sufficient – they did not need to trade. British merchants began secretly trading opium with Chinese merchants. The Chinese government begged the Queen to stop this trade but she refused – this resulted in the Opium War. Britain easily defeated China and forced them to sign the Treaty of Nanking. This treaty forced China to open up and trade with Britain.

Imperialism in Japan

Japan had also remained closed to trade with the outside world because they were self-sufficient. In 1853, Matthew Perry (an American) sailed to Japan. The Japanese saw the American ships and weapons and agreed to a treaty which opened Japan to trade with America. The Meiji (ruling family of Japan) took advantage of this situation and traded for goods that would industrialize and modernize Japan.

1. **Industrial Revolution** – movement in the 1800s that began in England; Machines replaced hand work

2. **Enclosure** – farmers in England in the 18th century began "enclosing their farms" to experiment with crops and animals

3. **Crop Rotation** – rotating crops to better land; resulted in larger harvest in the 1800s

4. **Entrepreneur** – person who begins a business

5. **Cotton Gin** – invented by Eli Whitney; made slavery an institution in American Southeast

6. **Union** –group of workers in the same industry that unite to push for higher pay and better working conditions

7. **Factory Act of 1833** – first law to protect child workers in England

8. **Mines Act of 1842** – piece of legislation passed in Great Britain in 1842 which was a response to the dangerous working conditions revealed in a Royal Commission report, set up by Sir Robert Peel

9. **Laissez-faire government** – belief that the government should not interfere in private business practices

10. **Water Frame** – patented by Richard Arkwright; spinning frame that could produce stronger threads for yarns; the first powered, automatic, continuous textile machine; enabled move away from home manufacturing towards factory production of textiles

11. **Spinning Jenny** – invented c 1764 by James Hargreaves; reduced amount of work needed to produce yarn; worker could produce eight or more spools at once

12. **John Kay** – patented a flying shuttle that increased the speed of the weaving process (1733)

13. **Eli Whitney** – inventor of the Cotton Gin and interchangeable parts

14. **James Watt** – made improvements to the steam engine

15. **George Stephenson** – English civil engineer and mechanical engineer, built first public railway line to use steam locomotives; Father of Railways

16. **Samuel Slater** – early American industrialist known as "Father of American Industrial Revolution" or "Father of American Factory System"

17. **Bourgeoisie** – upper middle class consisting of professionals and industrialists

18. **Boxer Rebellion** – Chinese revolt against western influence and presence; finally put down but not until the deaths of many Europeans within China

19. **Colonization** – act or process of establishing a colony or colonies

20. **Communism** – political and economic policy that supports no private property with all assets to be owned by the people as a group

21. **Suffrage** – the right to vote

22. **Realism** – movement which promotes looking at the world as it really exists

23. **Dual Monarchy** – government of Austria-Hungary where the emperor was recognized as the leader of both states yet each state had a separate parliament

24. **Corporation** – company which is owned by a number of individuals, all who have purchased stock

25. **Emigration** – to leave a country in order to reside in another

26. **Immigration** – enter a new country in order to set up residence

27. **Imperialism** – movement to dominate non-industrialized regions of the world in order to gain raw resources and have a ready market for manufacturing goods

28. **Kaiser** – emperor of Germany

29. **Muslim League** – political organization of India and Pakistan, founded in 1906 as the All-India Muslim League by Aga Khan III

30. **Opium War** – wars fought between China and Britain over the British trade in opium

31. **Proletariat** – urban working poor

32. **Protectorate** – relation of a strong state toward a weaker state or territory that it protects and partly controls

33. **Roosevelt Corollary** – declaration made by President Theodore Roosevelt in December 1904 authorizing the U.S. intervention of neighboring American countries in order to counter threats posed to U.S. security and interests

34. **Russo-Japanese War** – war between Russia and Japan over control of Chinese territories

35. **Second Reich** – second unification of Germany, after firsts Reich, which was the Holy Roman Empire (1871-1918)

36. **Seven Weeks War** – war between Prussia & Austria, Bavaria, Hanover, Saxony, and allied German states; resulted in Prussian Victory, also called Austro-Prussian War

37. **Socialism** – political and economic philosophy which supports the sharing of wealth

38. **Spanish-American War** – 1898, between U.S. and Spain; resulted in Spain ceding Puerto Rico, the Philippine Islands, and Guam to the U.S. and abandoning claims to Cuba

39. **Sphere of Influence** – territorial area over which political or economic influence is wielded by one nation

40. **Stock** – represents part ownership in a corporation

41. **Suez Canal** – man-made waterway which was built to join the Red Sea with the Mediterranean

42. **Third Republic** – French government 1870-1940, marked by social stability, industrialization, and establishment of a professional civil service

43. **Meiji Restoration** – post Tokugawa Shounate period in which the power of the Shogun was taken away in favor of the Emperor

44. **Taiping Rebellion** – most destructive civil war during the Qing dynasty; failed due to internal disagreement

45. **Romanticism** – literary movement which stressed following your emotions and heart to determine your actions

46. **The Eastern Question** – uncertainty of the fact of the failing Ottoman Empire

47. **Manifest Destiny** – idea that it is the natural right of the U. S. to stretch from the Atlantic to the Pacific

48. **Social Darwinism** – philosophy which supported an industrialized nation's right to dominate and abuse if desired another nation which is weaker

49. **Nationalism** – love and glorification of one's state

50. **Unification of Germany** – process in the late 19th century in which the 36 German states were unified under Prussian leadership

51. **Open Door Policy** – demand of the U.S. that China and Japan open their doors to the U.S. for trade

52. **Crimean War** – war in which France and Britain fought the Russians over the Russian encroachment into the Ottoman Empire

53. **Sino-Japanese War** – war between China and Japan over Korea

54. **Unificatino of Italy** – process in the late 19th century in which Piedmont-Sardinia's chancellor Count Camillo Cavour manipulated and militarily dominated the Italian city-states resulting in one united Italian state

55. **Karl Marx** – father of communism

56. **Bismarck** – Chancellor of Prussia who through the process of war and diplomatic policy united the German states of the Confederation into one united Germany

57. **Napoleon III** – emperor of the 2nd French Empire who was forced to abdicate as a result of the Franco-Prussian War

58. **Kipling** – famous English writer, 1865-1936, born in India, wrote the Jungle Book

59. **Boers** – Dutch colonists or descendants of Dutch colonists

60. **Zulu** – member of the Bantu people of southeast Africa, primarily inhabiting northeast Natal province in South Africa

61. **Matthew Perry** – U.S. Commodore who persuaded the Chinese and Japanese governments to open their doors to U.S. trade

62. **Theodore Roosevelt** – President of the United States, adopted the Roosevelt Corollary

63. **Liliuokalani** – Queen of the Hawaiian Islands, when she was deposed by those who sought annexation to the U.S. (1838-1917)

64. **Morse** – American artist, later invented the Morse code (1791-1872)

65. **Fulton** – built and sailed steam-engine powered Clermont, and another dozen similar steamships (1765-1815)

66. **Robert Owen** – wrote A New View of Society, established several utopian communities, Welsh manufacturer, set up innovative social and industrial welfare programs, including housing and schools for young children

67. **Robert Dale Owen** – U.S. social reformer, Representative in the U.S. House of Representatives, introduced a bill establishing the Smithsonian Institution, U.S. minister to Italy

68. **Friedrich Engels** – socialist who worked with Karl Marx on his history of communism

69. **Charles Darwin** – English botanist who developed the Theory of Evolution

70. **Wilheim I** – first emperor of a United Germany

71. **Sun-yat-Sen** – father of Chinese Nationalism

(Terms from GAVL, creative commons 3.0 [https://creativecommons.org/licenses/by/3.0/], http://cms.gavirtualschool.org/Shared/ SocialStudies/WorldHistory/ IndRevNationalismImperialism/KeyTerms.pdf)

A. Introduction

The key development of the Industrial Revolution was the application of machine power to replace men and animals. Favorable supplies of natural resources and the spur of population growth helped to produce the first Industrial Revolution in Britain. Industrialization built on the commercial advantages of Europe enjoyed in the world trade network and the developments of the scientific revolution.

B. Origins of Industrialization, 1770-1840

The initial inventions, such as James Watt's steam engine, that prompted the Industrial Revolution occurred in Britan. Each invention spawned new technological developments in related fields.

Transportation and communication innovations allowed products, people, and information to be moved more rapidly. Improved agricultural production fed the masses of workers who moved to the cities. Industrialization involved a shift in the organization of labor and the emergence of the factory system with its specialization of tasks and greater discipline. Industrialization also led to the creation of larger firms with greater access to capital and more advanced marketing techniques.

C. Spread of Industrialization

Britain's industrialization attracted imitators in the United States, Belgium, France, and Germany. The French Revolution promoted industrialization by sweeping away laws that restricted trade.

D. The Disruptions of Industrial Life

Industrialization promoted movement from the country to the city. Family life was disrupted in the process. Workers found themselves packed into slums and subjected to harsh labor conditions. Workers responded to new conditions, in some cases with outright resistance, but failed to slow the pace of technological change. Factory owners attacked popular leisure activities as a means of gaining greater control over the work force. Family patterns changed.

Lesson 104: Industrial Revolution Notes (cont.) World History

For the middle class, women retreated from the labor force to take up duties in the domestic household. Attitudes toward children involved greater concern for education and a sense of childhood.

E. The Revolutions of 1848

While not all governments sponsored the process of industrialization as fully as did Britain, most supported railway construction and technological fairs. Governments became more actively involved in supplying public education and improving slum conditions in the cities. Workers also began to become more active in the political process. In Britain, the Chartist movement attempted to democratize representation in the British Parliament. In some cases, unfulfilled labor requests contributed to revolutionary movements. Beginning in 1848, revolutions broke out throughout continental Europe. A revolution in France unseated the monarch and briefly instituted a republic. Workers groups pressed for social and economic reforms. Revolutions followed in Germany, Austria, and Hungary, where liberals and nationalists pressed for national unification.

Socialist and nationalist movements failed in 1848. Prussian and Austrian armies restored the status quo in central Europe. In France, a nationalist empire rapidly replaced the republic. The revolutions of 1848 were the last major European rebellions. Industrialization replaced the old social order with a new one. The aristocracy and artisan class declined after 1850 to be replaced by new social divisions between the middle-class laborers. The new social organization helped to make revolution obsolete.

(Adapted from GAVL, creative commons 3.0 [https://creativecommons.org/licenses/by/3.0/], https://cms.gavirtualschool.org/Shared/SocialStudies/WorldHistory/IndRevNationalismImperialism/IndustrialRevolutionReadingNotes.pdf)

Section 1: Italian Unification

Stirrings of Nationalism

Nationalism, or devotion to one's national group, was an important force in Europe during the 1800s. Greece, Belgium and Poland all fought for independence early in the century, sparking nationalist movements in Italy, Germany, Austria, and Russia.

One cause of the growth of nationalism was Europe's political boundaries. Most nations did not share a common language or culture. Instead, large empires included people of very different backgrounds. When the Congress of Vienna divided Italy, some parts falling under Austrian rule, nationalism grew. Some Europeans believed that people of the same background should form separate nation-states. **Guiseppe Mazzini** formed a nationalist group called Young Italy. Mazzini's group attracted tens of thousands of supporters who wanted to fight for the unification of the Italian states.

The Path Toward Unity

Politician **Camillo di Cavour** was a leader of the Italian unification movement. In 1847, Cavour founded a nationalist newspaper called Il Risorgimento, which means "resurgence" or "rebirth." Cavour believed that the Italian nationalist movement was strong enough to unite Italy, despite differences between the many Italian states.

In 1848, nationalist uprisings in France and Britain inspired a revolution in Italy. Some Italian states declared themselves republics. In other places, kings were forced to outline the people's rights in constitutions. In Piedmont, the king declared war against Austrian rule. Though the war ended in defeat, it was an important step toward unification. The leaders of the Italian states realized they needed to unite to defeat Austria.

Cavour became prime minister of the Kingdom of Sardinia in 1852. He formed an alliance with France during France's war against Russia. France, in turn, agreed to support Sardinia in its planned war against Austria. By 1860, the northern Italian states were liberated from the control of the Austrian Empire.

Garibaldi and the Red Shirts

An important member of Young Italy, **Guiseppe Garibaldi**, unified the southern Italian states and joined them to the north. Together, the states formed the Kingdom of Italy. In addition to military campaigns in central and southern Italy, Garibaldi is best known for his followers, the **Red Shirts**, who were named after their colorful uniforms.

Though Garibaldi wanted to establish a republic on conquered territory in Sicily, he instead offered it to King **Victor Emmanuel** of Sardinia. In 1860. all Italian territories except the Prussian state of Venetia and the French-supported Papal States voted for unification. But by 1870, Prussia gave Venetia to Italy, and France withdrew their troops from Italy. All of Italy was now unified.

Challenges After Unification

In the following years, Italy faced many challenges. People in the south resented that the government was located in the north. Rome became the new capital of Italy in 1871, but the Catholic Church did not recognize Italy as a legitimate nation. Catholics were forbidden from voting.

Voting rights increased and most Italian men could vote by the late 1800s. However, in the 50 years following unification, some 4.5 million Italians left Italy to escape widespread poverty. Working class Italians began to fight for change in a growing labor movement. Working conditions improved and production increased.

In 1882, Italy formed a military alliance with Austria-Hungary and Germany known as the **Triple Alliance**. Similar alliances brought most of Europe to war in 1914. Italy also tried to expand its influence elsewhere in the world. In 1911, Italy fought the Ottoman Empire and won territory in Africa.

Section 2: German Unification

Steps Toward Unification

Like Italy, Germany was not a unified nation in 1848. The German

Confederation was made up of 39 separate states that shared a language and culture. These states included Austria and Prussia. As revolution swept through Europe in 1848, liberal Germans protested for increased democracy. Prussian king **Frederick Wilhelm IV** promised a constitution and other reforms. However, by the end of 1848, the king went back on his promises.

Another early step toward creating a unified Germany was the **Zollverein** (TSOHL-fer-yn) in 1834. This economic alliance allowed for removal of taxes on products traded between the German states. The Zollverein encouraged the grown of railroads to connect the states. It helped join Germans economically, if not politically.

Bismarck's Plan for Germany

In 1862, **King Wilhelm I** chose **Otto von Bismarck** to be Prussia's prime minister. Bismarck became the leading force behind German unification, though unlike the revolutionaries of 1848, he did not believe in liberal democracy. His philosophy about government, **realpolitik**, was practical rather than idealistic, and based on the best interests of Prussia.

Bismarck declared that German unity would come by "blood and iron." When the parliament would not approve funds to expand the military, he fired them and collected his taxes anyway. Then, he built the Prussian army into a great war machine that could force Germany to unite.

In 1864, Bismarck formed a military alliance with Austria against Denmark, provoking a war. After a brief fight, Denmark gave up some territory, including a small bit of land in Prussia that came under Austrian control. Bismarck knew that conflict there would lead to what he desired: war between the two nations.

Unification and Empire

Convinced that war with Austria was coming, Bismarck promised territory to the Italian prime minister in return for his support. He also persuaded France to remain neutral in the upcoming war. Bismarck then provoked a war with Austria that lasted only seven weeks. Called the **Austro-Prussian War**, it resulted in a major victory for Prussia and the joining together of the North German states. It was the first step toward German unification.

In 1870, a conflict was brewing with France over the territory of Alsace and Lorraine. This issue sparked feelings of nationalism in the south German states. These states supported Prussia and the north German states in the **Franco-Prussian War** against France. Prussia won the war, and the peace treaty declared the unification of Germany. Wilhelm I became its first kaiser, or emperor. He appointed Bismarck as his first chancellor. The German victory brought more power to the new empire, while France's power decreased.

The Empire's Growth and Change

In the years after 1871, Germany became a strong empire. This period was known as the Second Reich. Each of Germany's 25 states wanted to retain some power. As a result, a federalist government developed so that power could be shared between state and national governments.

Germany also experienced economic growth after its unification. France paid reparations, money for damages, after the Franco-Prussian War. Germany used some of the money to build railroads to link the German states. Over the next 50 years, the German empire quickly caught up with the other industrial countries of Europe. However, German socialists protested against harsh factory conditions, and within a few years, Bismarck pushed for laws providing benefits for health, accidents, old age, and disability.

Bismarck believed that Germany was threatened by France. In response, he formed alliances with Austria-Hungary, Italy, and Russia. He also passed laws known as Kulturkampf, or "the struggle for culture," to limit the power of the Catholic Church in Germany.

In 1890, Bismarck was fired as prime minister after a disagreement with the kaiser. The kaiser continued to make alliances with other European nations.

Section 3: Austria-Hungary and the Ottoman Empire

The Austrian Empire

After the Congress of Vienna, the Austrian emperor, Franz I, and his foreign minister, Prince Metternich, worked together to maintain the power of the Austrian Empire and the Hapsburg monarchy. One way they did this was through laws known as the Carlsbad decrees that created a system of censorship and investigation of nationalist groups. In 1820, Metternich held the Congress of Troppau with several other European nations. Austria, Prussia, and Russia agreed to work together against nationalist revolutions in Europe. Great Britain and France refused.

In 1848, revolutions in France, Italy, and the German states set off revolts in the Austrian Empire. Metternich resigned due to rebellions in Vienna, and by the end of 1848, the emperor was replaced by **Franz Joseph I**.

Meanwhile, a revolution was raging in Hungary, another part of the Austrian empire. An ethnic group known as the **Magyars** fought for independence. The Russian czar sent troops to help Austria crush the revolt. Franz Joseph I then abolished the reforms enacted in 1848, including the new constitution. The revolutions stopped for a while.

The Dual Monarchy

As nationalist movements continued in Europe, Austria lost one of its provinces to Italy in 1859. When Prussia defeated Austria in 1866, Franz Joseph I decided to reach an agreement with Hungarian leaders. Called the Compromise of 1867, it created the **Dual Monarchy** of Austria-Hungary. In this agreement, Austria and Hungary became two separate, equal states, both ruled by the Austrian emperor.

The Dual Monarchy remained until 1918. The Dual Monarchy had both benefits and problems. Hungary provided raw materials and food to Austria. Austria provided industrial products to Hungary. Ethnic divisions remained among the countries who did not even speak the same language.

The Ottoman Empire

Many European powers were concerned about the declining Ottoman Empire. If it fell, other nations' territorial interests and the balance of power in Europe would be affected. The future of the Ottoman Empire became known as "The Eastern Question."

In 1854, the **Crimean War** erupted over a religious dispute between Catholics and Orthodox Christians in Palestine. Britain, France and the Ottoman Turks fought Russia in this deadly war that did not provide answers about the Ottoman Empire's future.

In 1865 and 1866, nationalist groups began revolutions in a small area of the empire called the Balkans. The rest of Europe became involved, and war broke out. The war lasted about two years and resulted in about 500,000 deaths. In the end, the Ottoman Empire suffered a major defeat and lost most of its territory.

In 1908, a nationalist group called the **Young Turks** began a revolution in Turkey. They fought against the absolute power of the sultan, the ruler of the Ottoman Empire. Their revolution resulted in a more representative, liberal government and more individual liberties for the Turkish people. Russia became involved in several conflicts against the Ottomans in the Balkans, hoping to gain territory. Great Britain, France, Germany, and Austria became involved in the **Balkan Wars**. By the end of these wars, the Ottoman Empire had lost most of its land in Europe.

Section 4: Unrest in Russia

Government and Society

Russia's social system and government differed from western European society. For centuries, Russian monarchs maintained absolute control over most aspects of Russian life. Most czars believed in autocracy, or government by one ruler with unlimited power. Russia's large size made this sort of rule effective. Its size also made Russia slower to industrialize than the rest of Europe. It had a mostly agricultural economy and most of the population was peasants. Many of these peasants were **serfs**, people who were considered part of the land they worked on and were ruled by lords, the wealthy nobles who owned the land. Serfs were not slaves, but their living conditions sometimes resembled slavery. Some czars had tried unsuccessfully to improve life for the serfs. The institution of serfdom was a major problem in Russian society.

Reform and Repression

Some Russians formed secret societies to fight against the czar. When Czar Alexander I died in 1825, a revolutionary group called the Decembrists rebelled against the government. Czar **Nicholas I**, who replaced Alexander I, crushed the rebellion and sent many of the Decembrists to Siberia. Although the revolt failed, it began a revolutionary movement that would not be stopped.

The next czar, **Alexander II**, believed that reform was necessary after Russia's defeat in the Crimean War. In 1861, he freed the Russian serfs, allowing them to buy the land on which they worked with their own money or with government help. Alexander II also set up a new judicial system, allowed some local self-government, and reorganized the army and navy.

The next czar, **Alexander III**, ended the reforms of his father and claimed absolute power for himself. At the same time, mobs of people were attacking and killing Jews in widespread violent attacks known as **pogroms**. Several waves of pogroms occurred in Russia.

The next czar, **Nicholas II**, led Russia in an era of great industrialization and expansion. The **Trans-Siberian Railroad** was built in the 1890s, linking western Russia with Siberia in the east. This expansion provoked a war with Japan known as the **Russo-Japanese War**, which began in 1904. The Japanese eventually defeated Russia.

War and Revolution

Russians who followed the communist theories of Karl Marx wanted a **socialist republic**. Under this society, there would be no private property, and the state would own and distribute all goods to the people. In 1902, a young Marxist named **Vladimir Lenin** published a work supporting the overthrow of the czar. Lenin became a leader of the growing revolutionary movement against the czars.

By 1905, many Russians were ready to rebel. On January 22, 1905, Orthodox priest Father Gapon led a group bringing a list of demands to the czar. As the protesters neared the Winter Palace, troops fired at the group, and hundreds died. The day became known as **Bloody Sunday**. This event inspired other Russians to rise up against the czar. Workers went on strike, university students formed protests, and peasants rebelled against their landlords. This was the Russian Revolution of 1905.

At first the Czar Nicholas II did not respond. Then he promised reform but did not follow through. Finally, a widespread worker's strike convinced him that something had to be done. He issued the October Manifesto, an official promise for reform and a more democratic government. It promised a Russian constitution that gave individual liberties to all Russians. He also gave voting rights to more Russian citizens who would elect representatives to the **Duma**, an assembly that would approve all laws.

(Adapted from GAVL, creative commons 3.0 [https://creativecommons.org/licenses/by/3.0/], https://cms.gavirtualschool.org/Shared/ SocialStudies/WorldHistory/IndRevNationalismImperialism/NationalismInEuropeAndRussiaReadingNotes.pdf)

Imperialism is the conquering and ruling of other lands. Imperialism greatly increased during the late 1800s.

World Climate During the 1800s

The political atmosphere was very tough and based in reality – called realpolitik. In 1861, Cavour led Italy into independence. In 1871, Germany became an independent country led by Bismarck. In America during this time period, westward expansion was taking place (they had already purchased the Louisiana Purchase from France) and the Civil War was being fought.

Economic Climate of the World

World trade grew by leaps and bounds after the Industrial Revolution because:
- Transportation between countries became easier: railroads were built and steamships made sea travel easy, plus they were large enough to carry trading items.
- Communication between countries improved: the telegraph made communications between businesses in different countries much easier and faster.
- Businesses began to grow larger: corporations were formed which allowed businesses to have a lot more money to operate with.
- Industry and business overtook farming as the key source of jobs for the public

Not All Changes Were Positive

With all of these changes came some negatives:
- Most factory and industry workers worked in horrible conditions (long hours, low pay, dangerous conditions).
- The business owners became very rich while the average worker remained poor – there was a huge gap between the rich and the poor.

Change in Workers' Attitudes
As a result of the gap between the rich and the poor, the working class began to demand more equality. Karl Marx wrote The Communist Manifesto which

outlined a new system called socialism which was supposed to equalize wealth within society. Socialists believed that all goods and services should be equally divided amongst the people – this way there was no rich and poor – everyone was equal.

Business Owners' Response to Socialism

Most business owners disagreed with the ideas of socialism and began to look for new sources of labor and new markets in which to sell their goods. This began the mass movement toward imperialism.

Imperialism

Until the late 1800s, Britain had always led the world in trade. With the Industrial Revolution, other countries began to catch up to Britain. Everyone began to believe that the key to economic domination was to have colonies. Several reasons led to this thinking:

1. Colonies provided new workers
2. Colonies provided new people to buy your goods/services
3. Europeans believed it was the "white man's burden" to go out and "civilize non-Europeans"

Imperialism took place in Africa, Asia, and Latin America.

Imperialism in Africa

European countries divided Africa into colonies. Africans were used to work in the mines mining gold, silver, and diamonds. Africans were forced to buy European goods and to pay large taxes to the Europeans. South Africa particularly supplied the Europeans with many diamonds that they could trade around the world.

Imperialism in South Asia (India)

India was very important to Europe because it possessed many natural resources. The British East India Company set up posts in India to gain natural resources and to sell their products. The Company became so powerful that they had their own army to protect their products (these Indian soldiers were called sepoys). Eventually, Britain began controlling India and taking its resources while heavily taxing all Indian citizens.

Imperialism in China

China was not interested in trade with the outside world because they were totally self-sufficient – they did not need to trade. British merchants began secretly trading opium with Chinese merchants. The Chinese government begged the Queen to stop this trade but she refused – this resulted in the Opium War. Britain easily defeated China and forced them to sign the Treaty of Nanking. This treaty forced China to open up and trade with Britain.

Imperialism in Japan

Japan had also remained closed to trade with the outside world because they were self-sufficient. In 1853, Matthew Perry (an American) sailed to Japan. The Japanese saw the American ships and weapons and agreed to a treaty which opened Japan to trade with America. The Meiji (ruling family of Japan) took advantage of this situation and traded for goods that would industrialize and modernize Japan.

Imperialism in Latin American

The United States focused their imperialistic efforts on Latin America. They built factories there and used laborers. They also sold US goods there – however, they never took colonies. The US built the Panama Canal to make trade easier. Later, the US began to focus their attention on the Pacific Islands as colonies.

1. **Entente** – "friendship" agreement between France, England and Russia

2. **Annex** – officially add a territory to a country

3. **Militarism** – when a country "glorifies" its military might

4. **Triple Alliance** – military alliance between Italy, Germany, and Austria-Hungary

5. **Triple Entente** – "friendship" agreement between France, England, and Russia

6. **Ultimatum** – "do this or else" statement

7. **Mobilize** – get troops and equipment in place for war

8. **Aggressor** – country that "starts" a war

9. **Neutrality** – official policy of not supporting any side or country in a war

10. **Schlieffen Plan** – Germany's plan for fighting a two-front war

11. **Central Powers** – Germany, Austria-Hungary, Ottoman Empire

12. **Allies** – Britain, Russia, France, and later the U.S.

13. **Western Front** – the area of military action in France and Belgium; trenches

14. **Battle of Marne** – first major battle of WWI; France stopped German advance here

15. **No-man's land** – deadly area between enemy trenches

16. **Trenches** – style of fighting on the Western Front in WWI

17. **U-boat** – Germany's "underwater boat;" submarine

18. **Total war** – when a war consumes a country's economy and social lives

19. **Rationing** – when the government determines how much goods you can have

20. **Propaganda** – government sponsored information; usually to sway public opinion

21. **Convoy** – U.S. strategy for protecting allied shipping against U-boat attacks

22. **Abdicate** – when a monarch "gives up" his or her throne

23. **Armistice** – an agreement to stop fighting

24. **Lusitania** – British cruise ship sunk by Germany in 1915; 129 Americans killed

25. **Self-determination** – the process by which a country determines its own statehood and forms its own allegiances and government

26. **Fourteen Points** – Woodrow Wilson's plan for peace after the war

27. **League of Nations** – permanent meeting of member nations to prevent war

28. **Reparations** – money owed to another country for war damages

29. **Big Three** – U.S. (Wilson); France (Clemenceau); England (George)

30. **Mandate** – order that some areas be controlled by the United Nations

31. **Zimmerman Note** – Germany promised Mexico some U.S. territory if Mexico would declare war against the U.S.

32. **William II** – last "Kaiser" or king of Germany; abdicated at the end of the war

33. **Woodrow Wilson** – President of the U.S. during WWI

34. **Franz Ferdinand** – Archduke of Austria-Hungary; his assassination in 1914 would start WWI

Anti-War/Neutrality

Lusitania

How and why did the USA get involved in the first World War?

Submarine Warfare

Zimmerman Note

Effect of US Involvement

Lesson 136: Years Between the Wars Terms

1. **Peter the Great** – Russian czar of the late seventeenth and early eighteenth centuries who tried to transform Russia from a backward nation into a progressive one by introducing customs and ideas from western European countries

2. **Catherine the Great** – empress of Russia in the late eighteenth century who encouraged the cultural influences of western Europe in Russia and extended Russian territory toward the Black Sea

3. **Serfs** – person in a condition of servitude, required to render services to a lord, commonly attached to the lord's land and transferred with it from one owner to another

4. **Autocracy** – government in which one person has uncontrolled or unlimited authority over others

5. **Nicholas I** – czar of Russia who suppressed the Decembrist movement and led Russia into the Crimean War

6. **Alexander II** – czar of Russia who emancipated the serfs in 1861

7. **Social democrats** – member of any certain Social Democratic parties

8. **Karl Marx** – German philosopher, economist, and revolutionary; wrote The Communist Manifesto with help & support of Friedrich Engels

9. **Lenin** – Russian founder of the Bolsheviks, leader of the Russian Revolution (1917); first head of USSR

10. **Bolsheviks** – member of the Russian Communist party (after 1918)

11. **Bloody Sunday** – 1905, Russian guards fired on an unarmed crowd or protesting citizens killing hundreds

12. **Duma** – council or official assembly

13. **Rasputin** – Siberian peasant monk who was very influential at the court of Czar Nicholas II and Czarina Alexandra

14. **Peace, Land, and Bread** – battle cry of the 1917 October Revolution that would change the history of Russia and affect the entire world

15. **Red Guard** – member of a Chinese Communist youth movement in the late 1960s, committed to the militant support of Mao Zedong

16. **White Army** – military arm of the White movement, loose coalition of anti-Bolshevik forces in the Russian Civil War

17. **Nationalist Party** – political party of the Republic of China (ROC); commonly known as Taiwan since the 1970s

18. **Trotsky** – Russian revolutionary and writer

19. **U.S.S.R** – Union of Soviet Socialist Republics

20. **Stalin** – Soviet political leader; secretary general of the Communist party

21. **Five Year Plan** – series of nation-wide centralized exercises in rapid economic development in the Soviet Union

22. **Command Economy** – economy that is planned and controlled by a central administration, as in the former Soviet Union

23. **Totalitarianism** – absolute control by the state or a governing branch of a highly centralized institution

24. **Mohandas Gandhi** – preeminent political and spiritual leader of India during the Indian independence movement

25. **Civil disobedience** – refusal to obey certain laws or governmental demands for the purpose of influencing legislation or government policy

26. **Non-violence** – absence or lack of violence; state or condition of avoiding violence

27. **Chiang Kai-Shek** – a political and military leader of 20th century China

28. **Mao Tse-Tung** – Chinese revolutionary, political theorist and communist leader of the People's Republic of China (PRC) from 1949 until his death 1976

29. **Red Army** – Soviet government's revolutionary militia beginning in the Russian Civil War of 1918-1922; grew into the national army of the USSR

30. **Long March** – massive military retreat undertaken by the Red Army of the Chinese Communist Party, forerunner of the People's Liberation Army, to evade the pursuit of the Kuomintang army

31. **Isolationism** – policy/doctrine of isolating one's country from the affairs of other nations by declining to enter into alliances; seeking to devote the entire efforts of one's country to its own advancement

32. **Albert Einstein** – theoretical physicist; many contributions to physics include special and general theories of relativity; founding of relativistic cosmology, first post-Newtonian expansion

33. **Sigmund Freud** – Austrian neurologist who founded psychoanalytic school of psychology

34. **Franz Kafka** – major fiction writer of the 20th century.

35. **Wall Street** – street in Lower Manhattan; first permanent home of the New York Stock Exchange

36. **Great Depression** – severe worldwide economic depression in the decade preceding World War II

37. **New Deal** – package of economic programs President Roosevelt effected between 1933 and 1935; the 3 R's goals: Relief to unemployed and hurt farms, Reform of business and financial practices, Recovery of economy during the Great Depression

38. **Franklin D. Roosevelt** – won his firsts of 4 presidential elections in 1932; combination of optimism and economic activism credited with keeping the country's economic crisis from devolving into political crisis; led U.S. through most of WWII

39. **Fascism** – governmental system led by a dictator having complete power

40. **Nazism** – principles or methods of the Nazis

41. **Antisemitism** – discrimination towards Jews

42. **Concentration Camps** – imprisonment or confinement of people, commonly in large groups, without trial

43. **Mussolini** – Italian politician who led the National Fascist Party; credited with being one of the key figures in the creation of fascism

44. **Adolf Hitler** – leader of the Nazis

45. **Nuremberg Laws** – anti-Semitic laws in Nazi Germany; introduced at the annual Nazi Party rally in Nuremberg

In 1917, a group named the Bolsheviks overthrew the czar of Russia and took control of the country for themselves. This is often called the Russian Revolution or the Bolshevik Revolution.

Causes of the Russian Revolution

1. Most Russians lived as serfs: Russia did not industrialize during the Industrial Revolution – it remained an agricultural country. 20% of people owned the land and the other 80% were serfs who worked the land. Serfs were treated like slaves.
2. Russians were required to pay large taxes.
3. Russians were not allowed to move freely within their own country – that had to get government permission to move.
4. Serfs/peasants were subject to the death penalty more frequently than wealthy Russians.
5. Russia was defeated in the Russo-Japanese War – this caused great casualties and humiliated the Russians.
6. Bloody Sunday: In January of 1905, many Russians marched to the czar's palace and demanded better living conditions. The czar's army fired on the crowd and killed 1000 people.
7. The czar focused too much attention on WWI and not enough on the problems within his own country.
8. Many serfs/peasants were living in poverty so severe that they couldn't even afford a loaf of bread.

The Bolsheviks

The Bolsheviks were led by Vladimir Lenin. They overthrew the czar and Lenin became the leader of Russia. He did three things to restore order to Russia:

1. He brutally crushed any group who tried to revolt against him – he created a climate of fear where no one dared to question him.
2. New Economic Policy: this allowed farmers to keep their surplus instead of giving it to the government. It allowed individuals to buy and sell goods for profit and it encouraged foreign trade.
3. Gave Russia the name the United Soviet Socialist Republics (USSR) which united all Russians together.

Lesson 140: Russian Revolution Notes

After Lenin died, Joseph Stalin became **dictator** (absolute ruler) of the USSR. Stalin made two major changes within the country:

1. Five Year Plan: this was meant to develop the economy – it gave control of all economic decisions to the government. Production of consumer goods was stopped and production of resource goods was increased. The government decided who worked, where they worked, when they worked and how much they got paid.

2. Agricultural Revolution: all farms were forced to join together into **collective farms** (farms worked by hundreds of families and owned by the government). This took all of the land away from the people and forced them to work for the government. If you refused, you were imprisoned and starved.

(Adapted from GAVL, creative commons 3.0 [https://creativecommons.org/licenses/by/3.0/], https://cms.gavirtualschool.org/Shared/SocialStudies/WorldHistory/YearsBetweenWars/RussianRevolutionReadingNotes.pdf)

Long Term Causes

Factor	Details
Oppression of the Serfs	
Class Inequalities	
Autocracy of Czars	
Defeat in Crimean War	
Rise of Marxism	

Immediate Causes

Factor	Details
Defeat in Russo-Japanese War	
Bloody Sunday	
Losses in World War I	
Indecision of Nicholas II	

Revolution

Factor	Details
Abdication of Nicholas II	
Failure of Provisional Government	
Growing Power of Soviets	
Return of Lenin to Russia	
Bolshevik takeover under Lenin	

Lesson 140: Russian Revolution Chart (cont.)   World History

Immediate Effects

Factor	Details
Civil War	
Peace with Germany under harsh treaty	
Bolshevik control of government	
Russian economy in ruins	

Long Term Effects

Factor	Details
Establishment of the Communist State	
Victory of Red Army in civil war	
New economic policy	
Formation of USSR	
Dictatorship under Communist Party	

Lesson 147: WWII Terms

1. **Nationalism** – extreme belief that one's country is better than another

2. **Fascism** – form of totalitarian government that promotes nationalism

3. **Totalitarianism** – government having total control over its citizens' lives

4. **Nazism** – fascist political party in Germany during the 1930s

5. **Neutrality Act** – act passed by the US in 1939 declaring our neutrality

6. **Appeasement** – policy of giving the aggressor nations that they wanted

7. **Blitzkreig** – Hitler's "lightning" style of war

8. **Non-aggression Pact** – Germany and Russia agreed not to fight over Poland

9. **Holocaust** – systematic killing of the Jews in Nazi Germany during WWII

10. **Genocide** – the attempt to wipe out an entire race of people

11. **Concentration Camps** – places where Jews were sent to work and die

12. **Axis Powers** – Japan, Italy, and Germany

13. **Allies** – France, Britain, Russia, and the United States

14. **V-E Day** – May 8, 1945; when Germany surrendered

15. **Kamikaze** – "Divine Wind;" name of Japanese suicide bombers in WWII

16. **Manhattan Project** – project that developed the first atomic bomb

17. **Yalta Conference** – meeting held in Feb.1945 to discuss post-war Europe

18. **Nuremberg Trials** – place Nazi war criminals were tried for war crimes

19. **Pearl Harbor** – US Naval base bombed by Japan on Dec 7, 1941

20. **Stalingrad** – turning point battle against Germany by the Russians

21. **D-Day** – the Allied invasion of Nazi occupied France in 1944

22. **Battle of the Bulge** – last offensive by the Nazis in 1944 before they surrendered

23. **Nagasaki** – second Japanese island where US dropped atomic bomb

24. **Hiroshima** – first Japanese island where US dropped atomic bomb

25. **Adolf Hitler** – Fascist dictator of Germany

26. **Hideki Tojo** – military dictator of Japan

27. **Winston Churchill** – Prime Minister of England during WWII

28. **Joseph Stalin** – Communist dictator of Russia during WWII

29. **Benito Mussolini** – Fascist dictator of Italy during WWII

30. **General Patton** – Major WWII American General

31. **Dwight Eisenhower** – commander of all Allied troops in Europe

32. **Harry Truman** – became President of the US in March of 1945

33. **Douglas McArthur** – commander of Allied troops in the Pacific

34. **Robert Oppenheimer** – leading scientist that helped develop atomic bomb

Years Between the Wars

Post World War I Europe was in shambles due to the massive destruction of human and economic resources. Once the smoke had cleared and the tally had been completed, it became obvious that Europe would need a major shot in the arm to recover emotionally and economically. Tremendous causalities (civilian and military), loss of resources, and virtual destruction of traditional cultural mores are just a few of the issues which emerged.

Perhaps the most significant post war event which developed was the signing of the Treaty of Versailles. This treaty held Germany responsible for the entire war. As a result, the new German government (Weimar Republic) was not able to recover politically and economically. The French and Belgium desire for revenge held the Germans to an indemnity it simply could not meet. The end result for Germany was the wholesale printing of German marks with no resource backing, creating a situation of hyperinflation in Germany.

It was this situation of national humiliation and economic punishment which paved the way for the rise of German Fascism. In addition to punishing Germany, the Allied powers rewrote the map of Europe creating new democracies as the great empires were dismantled.

This political restructuring created new democracies using ethnic identity and self-determination as the criteria. While this criteria for the redrawing of Europe seemed a good idea, the end result was that the European continent became even more unstable due to these new and unstable nations. Former colonial holdings by and large demanded independence from their controlling European state.

As World War I was to be the "war to end all wars," all considerations were made to create a political situation which would promote international peace. The Fourteen Points (a component of the Treaty of Versailles) were designed to address the issues and concepts which pushed the world into war: militarism, the alliance system, and Imperialism.

The end of the war also marked a shift in the social attitudes and values of societies around the world. Populations of the belligerent nations emerged from the war disillusioned due to economic chaos, mass casualties, and political impotence.

The Rise of Fascism

Fascism initially developed in Italy under the leadership of Benito Mussolini and later spread to Germany, adopted by Adolf Hitler's National Socialist Party. Fascism is characterized by a combination of intense nationalism and totalitarian leadership.

The Fascist Party was able to gain a majority in both Germany and Italy as the people were looking for strong, take-charge leadership, which was anticommunist.

While Mussolini turned out to be more talk than action, Hitler immediately began to act. He violated numerous terms of the Treaty of Versailles hoping the Allied nations would not challenge him, and he formed an alliance with Stalin of the USSR. Hitler invaded Poland in 1939, ultimately setting the stage for World War II.

World War II

World War II began when Germany, led by Hitler, invaded Poland, an action which was followed by the Soviet Union's invasion into eastern Poland and Finland. With that action, France and Britain declared war on Germany.

By summer of 1940, most of Europe had fallen to the German war machine, leaving only Great Britain to stand alone against the powerful nation. For six months, Britain was subject to daily air raids (Battle of Britain). Despite Britain's pleadings, the United States chose to stay out of the European conflict and didn't get involved in the conflict until the Japanese (allied to Germany) bombed Pearl Harbor.

The bombing of Pearl Harbor resulted in the United States declaring war on Japan followed by Germany (ally of Japan) declaring war on the U.S. At this point in the war, two fronts of conflict developed: the European Theatre and the Pacific Theatre.

The two major belligerents in the Pacific Theatre were the U.S. and the Japanese, creating a two-front war for the U.S. The Pacific Theatre was characterized by the military tactic of "island hopping," a strategy which called for the physical invasion and occupation of every other island in the South Pacific. These islands served as military bases which were critical for victory in the Pacific. When the U.S. was able to control two outer islands, the Japanese occupying the island in the middle would effectively be cut off. The Pacific war was a war on water and in the air. Therefore, aircraft carriers and island bases were extremely important to ultimate victory.

In 1941 the Germans invaded the Soviet Union, pushing the Soviets into the arms of the Allies. It is this action that many historians believe turned the tide of the war to the Allies. The "Big Three," the Soviet Union (Joseph Stalin), United States (Franklin Roosevelt), and Britain (Winston Churchill), dominated the Allied forces.

After the Allied invasions of Italy and Normandy, the western Allies squeezed from the north and the Soviets marched from the east toward Germany ultimately to encircle Berlin. In April 1945 after it had become clear that Germany was lost, Hitler committed suicide, enabling Germany to surrender. Tragically, Franklin Roosevelt died (succeeded by Harry Truman) shortly after Hitler and was never able to see the end of the war in Europe (VJE Day).

One of the tragic legacies of this war was the German attempt to wipe out the entire Jewish race (genocide) through mass extermination. This plan was known as the Final Solution and was well on its way to success by using death camps. Through these camps, some six million Jews had been murdered along with six million others who had been targeted by the Germans.

The war in the Pacific ended in the summer of 1945 as a result of the United States dropping atomic bombs on the Japanese cities of Hiroshima and Nagasaki.

Lesson 160: Cold War Terms

1. **Occupation Zone** – the area of central Germany occupied by the Soviet Union from 1945 on, at the end of WWII

2. **Superpower** – a state with a dominant position in the international system which has the ability to influence events and its own interests and project power on a worldwide scale to protect those interests

3. **Cold War** – state of conflict between nations that does not involve direct military action but is pursued primarily through economic and political actions, propaganda, acts of espionage or proxy wars waged by surrogates

4. **Buffer zone** – any zonal area that serves the purpose of keeping two or more other areas (often, but not necessarily countries) distant from one another, for whatever reason

5. **Nuclear weapon** – explosive device that derives its destructive force from nuclear reactions, either fission or a combination of fission and fusion

6. **Yalta Conference** – February 4-11, 1945, wartime meeting of the heads of government of the US, UK, and the Soviet Union for the purpose of discussing Europe's postwar reorganization

7. **United Nations** – international organization whose stated aims are facilitating cooperation in international law, international security, economic development, social progress, human rights, and achievement of world peace

8. **Universal Declaration of Human Rights** – declaration adopted by the United Nations General Assembly on 10 December 1948 in Paris

9. **Arms race** – (original usage) competition between two or more parties for the best armed forces

10. **Satellite** – an object which has been placed into orbit by human endeavor

11. **Iron Curtain** – symbolized the ideological fighting and physical boundary dividing Europe into two separate areas from the end of World War II in 1945 until the end of the Cold War in 1989.

12. **NATO** – an intergovernmental military alliance based on the North Atlantic Treaty which was signed on 4 April 1949

13. **Warsaw Pact** – informal name for the Treaty of Friendship, Cooperation and Mutual Assistance, created the Warsaw Treaty Organization

14. **Gross National Product** – market value of all goods and services produced in one year by labor and property supplied by the residents of a country

15. **European Union** – economic and political union of 27 member states which are located primarily in Europe

16. **De-Stalinization** – the process of eliminating the cult of personality and Stalinist political system created by Soviet leader Joseph Stalin

17. **Berlin Wall** – barrier constructed by the German Democratic Republic (GDR, East Germany) starting on 13 August 1961, that completely cut off West Berlin from surrounding East Germany and from East Berlin

18. **Solidarity** – integration, and degree and type of integration, shown by a society or group with people and their neighbors

19. **Marshall Plan** – primary program of the United States for rebuilding and creating a stronger economic foundation for the countries of Europe

20. **Truman Doctrine** – policy set forth by US President Harry Truman stating that the US would support Greece and Turkey with economic and military aid to prevent their falling into the Soviet sphere

21. **Bay of Pigs Invasion** – unsuccessful attempt by a CIA-trained force of Cuban exiles to invade southern Cuba with support from US government armed forces to overthrow the Cuban government of Fidel Castro

22. **Cuban Missile Crisis** – confrontation between the Soviet Union, Cuba, and the United States in October 1962, during the Cold War

23. **Tiananmen Square** – large city square in the center of Beijing, China, named after the Tiananmen Gate

24. **Margaret Thatcher** – served as Prime Minister of the United Kingdom from 1979 to 1990 and Leader of the Conservative Party from 1975 to 1990

25. **Nikita Krushchev**– led the Soviet Union during part of the Cold War

26. **Mikhail Gorbachev** – reforming Soviet Union Premier in the 1980s

27. **Leonid Brezhnev** – was the General Secretary of the Central Committee of the Communist Party of the Soviet Union, presiding over the country from 1964 until his death in 1982

28. **Fidel Castro** – a Marxist Cuban leader

29. **Apartheid** – set of racially discriminatory laws on the majority black population of South Africa

Building the Cold War World

1. Contest between capitalism and communism

    a. U.S. ideology: liberalism, property rights, free market, welfare state

    b. Khrushchev's reformed communism: relaxation of terror, economic growth

2. Global communism containment

    a. Against the spread of communism, U.S. fashioned *containment* strategy

    b. Soviet counter-strategies: support for national liberation, military parity with U.S.

3. A divided Germany

    a. Europe was divided into two blocs along with two superpowers

    b. West and East Germany were formed in 1949

    c. To prevent refugees to West Germany, Berlin Wall and fortification on border were reinforced

4. Nuclear arms race

    a. Creation of NATO and Warsaw Treaty Organization initiated arms race

    b. By 1960s, USSR reached military parity with U.S.

    c. By 1970 both superpowers acquired MAD

Confrontation in Korea and Cuba and Vietnam

1. Korean War

    a. The 38th parallel of latitude divided Korea (1948)

    b. North Korean troops crossed the 38th parallel, captured Seoul (June 1950)

    c. U.S. and UN troops pushed back North Korean troops, captured Pyongyang

    d. Chinese troops came in, pushed U.S. forces and their allies back in the south

e. Both sides agreed to cease fire in July, 1953

2. Globalization of containment
   a. Creation of SEATO, an Asian counterpart of NATO
   b. Eisenhower's famous "domino theory"

3. Cuba: Nuclear Flashpoint
   a. Castro's revolutionary force overthrew Batista's autocratic rule, 1959
   b. Castro expropriated U.S. properties, killed or exiled thousands of political opponents
   c. U.S. cut off Cuban sugar imports, imposed export embargo
   d. Castro accepted Soviet massive economic aid and arms shipments
   e. Bay of Pigs fiasco (April, 1961) diminished U.S. prestige in Latin America
   f. To protect Castro's regime, USSR assembled nuclear missiles on Cuba, 1962
   g. Kennedy's public ultimatum called on Soviets to withdraw all missiles
   h. USSR yielded to US demand, Kennedy pledged to overthrow Castro

4. Vietnam
   a. United States attempts to stop communist guerillas (Viet Cong) in Vietnam from establishing a communist-run government (1965-1975)
   b. Though never directly fought with USSR, it was no secret the USSR was supplying the Viet Cong
   c. In 1975, after 70,000 U.S. casualties, American soldiers pull out of Vietnam and communist government is established

The Chinese Communist Revolution was the key defining period of modern China, and therefore one of the most important grouping of events of the 20th Century. By establishing a Communist regime under Mao Zedong in mainland China, and a rump Nationalist regime under Chiang Kai-Shek on Taiwan, the Revolution had ramifications that continue to define the modern world.

Misconceptions

The Chinese Communist Revolution is often confused with the larger Chinese Civil War. The latter was a much larger struggle which began in 1927, and continued until at least 1950. The Chinese Communist Revolution refers specifically to the latter stages of that contest.

By some reckonings, the Chinese Civil War did not end until the Republic of China (Taiwan) unilaterally declared it over in 1991, but as the People's Republic of China never acknowledged this and there has never been a peace treaty of any kind, strictly speaking the Chinese Civil War could be considered as dormant, but not over.

Time Frame

The Communist Revolution began with the 1946 resumption of open war between the Communist Party of China and the Kuomintang (KMT), or Chinese Nationalists, after the end of the Second World War. It concluded with the effective victory of the Communists and the expulsion of Nationalist forces to the island of Taiwan.

History

With the end of the Second World War, the energies of the Communists and the KMT were no longer focused on fighting the Japanese. The 1946 breakdown of peace talks led to the resumption of hostilities, with the Soviet Union providing Mao Zedong's Communists with support, and the KMT of Chiang Kai-Shek backed by the United States.

Initially the KMT sought to make the frontline of the war in Manchuria, however it was an unequal struggle. The KMT forces had borne the brunt of the conflict with the Japanese, and were largely exhausted by the effort. Contrary to later claims made by Maoists propagandists, the Communists did very little to expel the Japanese from China and were content to save their strength for a later resumption of the civil war. The Nationalists were also hamstrung by their own corruption and the failure of their economic management, which made them deeply unpopular across China.

The Communists suffered defeats and setbacks in 1946 and 1947, but learned from their errors and by 1948 had turned the tables on the KMT, defeating them in battle and capturing large amounts of demoralized troops and their equipment. Beijing fell in 1949 with hardly a shot fired in its defense. Mao Zedong formally proclaimed the People's Republic of China a reality in October 1949. Chian Kai-Shek retreated with the remainder of his army and roughly two million refugees to Taiwan, and subsequently repelled from outlying islands at the Battle of Kuningtou, but the Communists captured Hainan Island in 1950. With the capture of Hainan, the lines ossified and the Chinese Communist Revolution ended.

Effects

For more than twenty years after the Communist Revolution, the West blocked any change in the UN Security Council that would allow the Communist People's Republic of China to replace the Nationalist Republic of China as the veto-wielding permanent member. This did not change until Nixon and his famous rapprochement with the Communist Chinese.

Less than one year after the end of the Chinese Communist Revolution, Chinese troops would be battling UN forces in the Korean War. Communist victory in the world's most populous country also fanned the anti-communist hysteria of 1950s America, and the question "who lost China?" would figure prominently in the accusations of Senator Joseph McCarthy and others.

Significance

The Chinese Revolution was among the first hot conflicts of the Cold War, and its ramifications were certainly among the most far reaching. The most important long-term effect was to create a Communist state with the size and power to stand as a rival to the Soviet Union within the Communist world. The Soviets and Chinese were initially allies, but eventually split apart, and fought bloody border conflicts in the 1960s. The Sino-Soviet split forced many Communist states to choose sides, with China even invading pro-Soviet Vietnam in 1979.

1. **Margaret Thatcher** – First female Prime Minister of England

2. **Indira Gandhi** – First female Prime Minister of India

3. **Golda Meir** – first female Prime Minister of Israel

4. **Al Qaeda** – terroristic organization led by Osama bin Laden

5. **Hamas** – terroristic political organization that wants to establish an independent Palestinian nation and wipe Israel off the map

6. **United Nations** – organization of most of the world's nations formed after WWII

7. **World Trade Organization (WTO)** – international organization that regulates trade between many of the world's countries

8. **OPEC** – organization of the world's oil producing nations; primarily made up of middle eastern nations

9. **Global Warming** – controversial and debatable theory that the earth is warming due to pollution by man

10. **Greenhouse Effect** – a process by which thermal radiation from a planetary surface is absorbed by atmospheric greenhouse gases, and is re-radiated in all directions. Since part of this re-radiation is back towards the surface, energy is transferred to the surface and the lower atmosphere. As a result, the temperature there is higher than it would be if direct heating by solar radiation were the only warming mechanism.

11. **Ozone Layer** – a layer in Earth's atmosphere which contains relatively high concentrations of ozone (O_3). This layer absorbs 97-99% of the Sun's high frequency ultraviolet light, which is potentially damaging to life on Earth. It is mainly located in the lower portion of the stratosphere from approximately 13 km to 40 km above Earth, though the thickness varies seasonally and geographically. The ozone layer was discovered in 1913 by the French physicists Charles Fabry and Henri Buisson.

12. **Fossil Fuel** – fuels formed by natural resources such as anaerobic decomposition of buried dead organisms. The age of the organisms and their resulting fossil fuels is typically millions of years, and sometimes exceeds 650 million years. The fossil fuels, which contain high percentages of carbon, include coal, petroleum, and natural gas. Fossil fuels range from volatile materials with low carbon: hydrogen ratios like methane, to liquid petroleum to nonvolatile materials composed of almost pure carbon, like anthracite coal. Methane can be found in hydrocarbon fields, alone, associated with oil, or in the form of methane clathrates. It is generally

accepted that they formed from the fossilized remains of dead plants and animals by exposure to heat and pressure in the Earth's crust over millions of years.

13. **Acid Rain** – a rain or any other form of precipitation that is unusually acidic, i.e. elevated levels of hydrogen ions (low pH). It can have harmful effects on plants, aquatic animals, and infrastructure through the process of wet deposition. Acid rain is caused by emissions of compounds of ammonium, carbon, nitrogen, and sulphur, which react with the water molecules in the atmosphere to produce acids.

14. **Internet** – a global system of interconnected computer networks that use the standard Internet Protocol Suite (TCP/IP) to serve billions of users worldwide. It is a network of networks that consists of millions of private, public, academic, business, and government networks, of local to global scope, that are linked by a broad array of electronic and optical networking technologies. The Internet carries a vast range of information resources and services, such as the inter-linked hypertext documents of the World (WWW) and the infrastructure to support electronic mail.

15. **Global Economy** – refers to the economy, which is based on economies of all of the world's countries, national economies. In addition, global economy can be seen as the economy of global society and national economies - as economies of local societies, making the global one. It can be evaluated in various kinds of ways. For instance, depending on the model used, the valuation that is arrived at can be represented in a certain currency, such as 2006 US dollars.

(Terms from GAVL, creative commons 3.0 [https://creativecommons.org/licenses/by/3.0/], http://cms.gavirtualschool.org/Shared/ SocialStudies/ WorldHistory_15/WH_GlobalIssuesShared/GlobalIssues_KeyTerms.pdf)

Made in the USA
Coppell, TX
19 July 2025

52073848R00077